"This wonderful book is a gift to us all. The editors have done a superb job of bringing together a collection of articles on a fascinating and much neglected topic that are as informative as they are delightful. By exploring the psychological aspects of sports, this book breaks new ground and does so in a way that enriches our understanding of both fields. For sports enthusiasts and all those in the mental health field who have an interest in sports, this is a book to savor and enjoy."
– Theodore Jacobs M.D., Training and Supervising Analyst, New York Psychoanalytic Institute

"At long last, psychoanalysts take a serious and respectful look at sports and sports devotees, both as participants and fans. This long overdue book, authored by sophisticated and experienced psychoanalysts acknowledges sports (play?) as an integral part of life, and a bellwether for understanding gender assembly, group and mob dynamics, and, above all, *passion*—that irrational impulse that makes our lives meaningful. As contemporary psychoanalytic inquiries tend to do, it conflates the teller with the tale so one also gets a glimpse of the authors' own experience in sports. It is an original, readable and informative volume and I would heartily recommend it to colleagues and a general audience alike."
– Edgar Levenson, M.D., Fellow Emeritus, Training; Supervisory Analyst and Faculty, William Alanson White Institute

"In a refreshing move outside the consulting room, Hirsch, Blumberg, and Watson invite us to contemplate the dynamic element embedded in the physical—and the observing of the physical. Essays written by eminent male and female analysts ask us to consider sports from an analytic point of entrée: What do sports do for us? Why do we play? Why do we watch and cheer? Engaging for the avid player, fan and those not involved with sports at all, this book addresses the intersection of psychodynamics and the passionate involvements we use to get away from our ordinary selves."
– Joyce Slochower, Ph.D., Adjunct Professor of Psychology and Supervisor, NYU Postdoctoral Program in Psychotherapy and Psychoanalysis

Psychoanalytic Perspectives On Intense Involvement in Sports

This book is a unique volume that brings a variety of psychoanalytic perspectives to the study of sport. It highlights the importance of sports for different individuals and how the function and use of sports can be brought into the consulting room.

Passionate interest in actively engaging in sports is a universal phenomenon. It is striking that this aspect of human life, prior to this volume, has received little attention in the literature of psychoanalysis. This edited volume is comprised largely of psychoanalysts who are themselves avidly involved with sports. It is suggested that intense involvement in sports prioritizes commitment and active engagement over passivity and that such involvement provides an emotionally tinged distraction from the various misfortunes of life. Indeed, the ups and downs in mood related to athletic victory or defeat often supplant, temporarily, matters in life that may be more personally urgent. Engaging in sports or rooting for teams provides a feeling of community and a sense of identification with like-minded others, even among those who are part of other communities and have sufficient communal identifications.

This book offers a better psychoanalytic understanding of sports to help us discover more about ourselves, our patients and our culture, and will be of great interest to psychotherapists and psychoanalysts, or anyone with an interest in sport and its link to psychoanalysis and mental health.

Irwin Hirsch, Ph.D., supervises and teaches at the Manhattan Institute for Psychoanalysis, the William Alanson White Institute and the NYU Postdoctoral Program and at other psychoanalytic institutes nationally.

Phillip Blumberg, Ph.D., is a faculty member and supervisor at the William Alanson White Institute and Adjunct Associate Professor in the doctoral program in Clinical Psychology at Teachers College, Columbia University.

Robert I. Watson, Jr., Ph.D., is a supervising psychoanalyst at the William Alanson White Institute and faculty member at the Institute for Contemporary Psychotherapy.

Psychoanalysis In A New Key Book Series

Donnel Stern
Series Editors

When music is played in a new key, the melody does not change, but the notes that make up the composition do: change in the context of continuity, continuity that perseveres through change. Psychoanalysis in a New Key publishes books that share the aims psychoanalysts have always had, but that approach them differently. The books in the series are not expected to advance any particular theoretical agenda, although to this date most have been written by analysts from the Interpersonal and Relational orientations.

The most important contribution of a psychoanalytic book is the communication of something that nudges the reader's grasp of clinical theory and practice in an unexpected direction. Psychoanalysis in a New Key creates a deliberate focus on innovative and unsettling clinical thinking. Because that kind of thinking is encouraged by exploration of the sometimes surprising contributions to psychoanalysis of ideas and findings from other fields, Psychoanalysis in a New Key particularly encourages interdisciplinary studies. Books in the series have married psychoanalysis with dissociation, trauma theory, sociology, and criminology. The series is open to the consideration of studies examining the relationship between psychoanalysis and any other field—for instance, biology, literary and art criticism, philosophy, systems theory, anthropology, and political theory.

But innovation also takes place within the boundaries of psychoanalysis, and Psychoanalysis in a New Key therefore also presents work that reformulates thought and practice without leaving the precincts of the field. Books in the series focus, for example, on the significance of personal values in psychoanalytic practice, on the complex interrelationship between the analyst's clinical work and personal life, on the consequences for the clinical situation when patient and analyst are from different cultures, and on the need for psychoanalysts to accept the degree to which they knowingly satisfy their own wishes during treatment hours, often to the patient's detriment. A full list of all titles in this series is available at: https://www.routledge.com/series/LEAPNKBS

Psychoanalytic Perspectives On Intense Involvement in Sports

Edited by Irwin Hirsch, Phillip Blumberg and Robert I. Watson, Jr.

LONDON AND NEW YORK

First published 2021
by Routledge
2 Park Square, Milton Park, Abingdon, Oxon OX14 4RN

and by Routledge
52 Vanderbilt Avenue, New York, NY 10017

Routledge is an imprint of the Taylor & Francis Group, an informa business

© 2021 selection and editorial matter, Irwin Hirsch, Phillip Blumberg and Robert I. Watson, Jr.; individual chapters, the contributors

The right of Irwin Hirsch, Phillip Blumberg and Robert I. Watson, Jr. to be identified as the authors of the editorial material, and of the authors for their individual chapters, has been asserted in accordance with sections 77 and 78 of the Copyright, Designs and Patents Act 1988.

All rights reserved. No part of this book may be reprinted or reproduced or utilised in any form or by any electronic, mechanical, or other means, now known or hereafter invented, including photocopying and recording, or in any information storage or retrieval system, without permission in writing from the publishers.

Trademark notice: Product or corporate names may be trademarks or registered trademarks, and are used only for identification and explanation without intent to infringe.

British Library Cataloguing-in-Publication Data
A catalogue record for this book is available from the British Library

Library of Congress Cataloging-in-Publication Data
Names: Hirsch, Irwin, editor. | Blumberg, Phillip, editor. | Watson, Robert I., 1947- editor.
Title: Psychoanalytic perspectives on intense involvement in sports / edited by Irwin Hirsch, Phillip Blumberg and Robert I. Watson Jr.
Description: Abingdon, Oxon ; New York, NY : Routledge, 2021. | Series: Psychoanalysis in a new key | Includes bibliographical references and index.
Identifiers: LCCN 2020019454 (print) | LCCN 2020019455 (ebook) | ISBN 9780367542412 (hardback) | ISBN 9780367542382 (paperback) | ISBN 9781003088295 (ebook)
Subjects: LCSH: Sports–Psychological aspects. | Athletes–Psychology. | Sports spectators–Psychology. | Psychoanalysis.
Classification: LCC GV706.4 .P6664 2021 (print) | LCC GV706.4 (ebook) | DDC 796.01/9–dc23
LC record available at https://lccn.loc.gov/2020019454
LC ebook record available at https://lccn.loc.gov/2020019455

ISBN: 978-0-367-54241-2 (hbk)
ISBN: 978-0-367-54238-2 (pbk)
ISBN: 978-1-003-08829-5 (ebk)

Typeset in Times
by Swales & Willis, Exeter, Devon, UK

Irwin Hirsch, Ph.D.

For my grandchildren, Aurelie, Ana, Theo and Dilan, and the pleasure and camaraderie that sports brings them.

Phillip Blumberg, Ph.D.

In memory of Ted Ashley, Verna Bloom, Edward Glantz, and Stanley and Laura Kauffmann who all taught me the true meaning of play.

Robert I. Watson, Jr., Ph.D.

For my family, Jane, Mark, and Joanna, who have kept alive my passion for sports through both participation and being devoted fans.

The editors wish to thank Taylor & Francis, Routledge, and *Contemporary Psychoanalysis* for permission to republish the following articles from *Contemporary Psychoanalysis*, Volume 46, Number 4, Fall 2010:

Adrienne Harris (2010) Baseball's Bisexuality, pp. 480–503.
W. B. Carnochan (2010) The Faith of the Fan, pp. 504–509.
Steve Cooper (2010) Some Reflections on the Romance and Degradation of Sports, pp. 510–522.
Howard M. Katz (2010) The Athlete's Dream, pp. 523–538.
James Hansell (2010) Sports – Applied Psychoanalysis *Par Excellence*, pp. 539–549.
Don Greif (2010) Revaluing Sports, pp. 550–561.
Stephen Seligman (2010) The Sensibility of Baseball, pp. 562–577.
Jean Petrucelli (2010) Serve, Smash, and Self-States, pp. 578–588.

Contents

Acknowledgements	xiii
List of contributors	xv
Introduction: on intense involvement with sports IRWIN HIRSCH, PH.D.	1

Psychoanalytic perspectives on intense involvement in sports   9

1 Baseball's bisexuality ADRIENNE HARRIS, PH.D.	11
2 Some reflections on the romance and degradation of sports: watching and metawatching in the changing transitional space of sport STEVEN COOPER, PH.D.	36
3 Revaluing sports DON GREIF, PH.D.	50
4 The sensibility of baseball: structure, imagination, and the resolution of paradox STEPHEN SELIGMAN, D.M.H.	62
5 Serve, smash, and self-states: tennis on the couch and courting Steve Mitchell JEAN PETRUCELLI, PH.D.	80

A psychoanalytic look at sports fandom 93

6 The faith of the fan 95
W. B. CARNOCHAN, PH.D.

7 A relational view of passion in sports and the group experience 102
ROBERT I. WATSON, JR., PH.D.

8 Sports—applied psychoanalysis: *par excellence* 112
JAMES HANSELL, PH.D.

Sports and psychoanalytic therapy 125

9 Early adolescence and the search for idealization through basketball and its celebrities: a developmental perspective 127
CHRISTOPHER BONOVITZ, PSY.D.

10 The athlete's dream 144
HOWARD M. KATZ, M.D.

11 Recommend aerobic activity to our patients? One psychoanalyst's perspective 161
JOHN V. O'LEARY, PH.D.

12 Marathons, mothering, and the maelstrom of trauma: running away with yourself 176
STEPHANIE ROTH-GOLDBERG, LCSW-R, CEDS

Index 187

Acknowledgements

I am deeply grateful to my two co-editors and friends, who, as part of a cohesive team, are responsible for bringing this book to fruition. I will always be happy to be their teammates.

Involvement in sports, both as participant and fan, has been responsible for a high percentage of the friends I have had since childhood. Many of these friends have been casual, often passing, though some have endured for many, many years. I wish to acknowledge all of them. Engagement in sports, in addition to the pleasure this has given me, was initially a vehicle to separate from my loving but insular family and to enter a rich and exciting social world. This sports-tinted social world remains a part of my life and as well, has become an element in my cherished relationships with my children and grandchildren.

I can't conclude without a tribute to my beloved Brooklyn Dodgers, unquestionably one of the profound loves of my life.

Irwin Hirsch, Ph.D.

I want to thank Andrea, Julie, and Adam Hansell for their assistance as well Mark Blechner, Susan Fabrick, Emmanuel Fiano, Ruth Livingston, and Donnel Stern for their editorial advice and encouragement.

Phillip Blumberg, Ph.D.

I am truly appreciative of my two friends and editors who encouraged my work on this book from its inception. Without their original work and their dedication there would not be this volume.

I have been interested in sports since my childhood. I grew up in the Midwest, and sports were part of the everyday fabric of life. I was lucky enough to participate in team sports in both high school and college, which solidified my interest. As years passed, participation as an athlete diminished, but I was able to channel my interest into coaching for both my son's and daughter's teams. These teams gave us all a chance to bond in a different way. Our bond has continued by our all being committed fans of the outstanding New York Yankees.

This volume has given me the chance to bring together two of the great interests of my life, sports and psychoanalysis. I hope it demonstrates how psychoanalytic thinking can be applied to this very important aspect of many people's lives.

I would like to thank Donnel Stern, editor of this series, for all his encouragement and help in producing this book. Also, without the Viceroys, my peer supervision group, I would never have had the confidence to do the work necessary for this book. Thank you greatly Mark, Annie, Sandy, Richard, and John. Most importantly I want to thank my wife Jane, who was the best athlete in the family, and who aided me through her encouragement and editing to produce this volume.

Robert I. Watson, Jr., Ph.D.

Contributors

Phillip Blumberg, Ph.D., is on the Faculty of the William Alanson White Psychoanalytic Institute and adjunct Associate Professor of Clinical Psychology at Columbia University. He has served on the editorial board of the *Journal of the American Psychoanalytic Association*, associate editor and book review editor of *Contemporary Psychoanalysis*, and on the executive committee of the Helix Center at the New York Psychoanalytic Institute.

Christopher Bonovitz, Psy.D., Faculty, Supervising and Training Analyst, William Alanson White Institute. Clinical Associate Professor of Psychology and Clinical Consultant, New York University (NYU) Postdoctoral Program in Psychotherapy and Psychoanalysis. Associate Editor, *Psychoanalytic Dialogues* and the *Journal of Contemporary Psychoanalysis*. Co-authored an edited book with Andrew Harlem entitled *Developmental Perspectives In Child Psychoanalysis and Psychotherapy*, Routledge (2018).

W. B. Carnochan, Ph.D., Lyman Professor of the Humanities, emeritus, Stanford University, where until retirement he taught British literature of the eighteenth century. Among his Books, *Confessions of a Dodger Fan* (2013) describes his own "strange experience of fandom."

Steven Cooper, Ph.D., Training and Supervising Analyst, Boston Psychanalytic Society and Institute. Associate Professor of Psychology in Psychiatry at Harvard Medical School. Joint Editor-in-Chief of *Psychoanalytic Dialogues* from 2007–2012; now Chief Editor Emeritus. Author of *Objects of Hope, A Disturbance in the Field: Essays in Transference-Countertransference*, and *The Analyst's*

Experience of the Depressive Position: The Melancholic errand of Psychoanalysis.

Don Greif, Ph.D., Faculty and Supervisor at William Alanson White Institute. Emeritus Editor of Contemporary Psychoanalysis. Psychologist/psychoanalyst with a private psychotherapy, forensic and sports psychology practice in New York City.

James Hansell Ph.D., (1955–2013), was director of clinical training for the Professional Psychology program at George Washington University. He was previously on the faculties of the Michigan Psychoanalytic Institute and the University of Michigan Departments of Psychology and Psychiatry. While at Michigan he was a consulted by the women's soccer and gymnastics teams.

Adrienne Harris, Ph.D., Faculty and Supervisor at New York University Postdoctoral Program in Psychotherapy and Psychoanalysis and at the Psychoanalytic Institute of Northern California. Editor at *Psychoanalytic Dialogues*, and *Studies In Gender and Sexuality*. In 2009, she, Lewis Aron, and the late Jeremy Safran established the Sandor Ferenczi Center at the New School University.

She co-edits the Book Series: Relational Perspectives in Psychoanalysis, a series now with over 90 published volumes.

Irwin Hirsch, Ph.D., Supervisor and/or faculty at The Manhattan Institute for Psychoanalysis; The William Alanson White Institute; The NYU Postdoctoral Program in Psychotherapy and Psychoanalysis, and the National Program at The National Institute for Psychotherapies. He is on the Editorial Boards of *Contemporary Psychoanalysis*, *Psychoanalytic Dialogues*, and *Psychoanalytic Perspectives*. He is author or editor of 5 psychoanalytic books and over 90 journal articles and book chapters.

Howard M. Katz, M.D., is a Training and Supervising Psychoanalyst at Boston Psychoanalytic Society and Institute, and is a Lecturer in Psychiatry, Harvard Medical School.

John V. O'Leary, Ph.D., Faculty and Supervisor at William Alanson White Institute. Member of Division 39, American Psychological Association. He is the author of many book chapters and articles, his interests include psychopathology (paranoia and depression), neuro psychoanalysis, relational group therapy, and the impact of social issues (income inequality, racism and classism) on the practice of psychoanalysis.

Jean Petrucelli, Ph.D., Faculty, Supervising and Training Analyst, William Alanson White Institute. Faculty, Director and Co-Founder of the Eating Disorders, Compulsions & Addictions Services (EDCAS), started in 1995 and became Founder and Director of the one-year certificate training program in eating disorders, compulsions and addictions, which started in 2006. She is Chair of the Conference Advisory Board (CAB), William Alanson White Institute; adjunct clinical Professor and Co-Chair of the IH Track Faculty and Curriculum committee at NYU Postdoctoral Program in Psychotherapy and Psychoanalysis; adjunct faculty, Institute for Contemporary Psychotherapy (ICP); Associate Editor, *Contemporary Psychoanalysis*. She is editor of five books, including *Body States: Interpersonal and Relational Perspectives on the Treatment of Eating Disorders*, Routledge (2015), for which she won the American Board & Academy of Psychoanalysis 2016 edited book award. She also has a private practice in New York City.

Stephanie Roth-Goldberg, LCSW, is an eating disorder psychotherapist in New York City and the founder of Intuitive Psychotherapy NYC, a small private group practice. She is a candidate in the Division 1 Psychoanalytic training program at the William Alanson White Institute.

Stephen Seligman, D.M.H., Clinical Professor of Psychiatry at the University of California, San Francisco and the New York University Postdoctoral Program in Psychanalysis. Joint Editor-in-Chief of *Psychoanalytic Dialogues*. Training and Supervising Analyst, San Francisco Center for Psychoanalysis and Psychoanalytic Institute of Northern California. Author of *Relationships in Development: Infancy, Intersubjectivity, Attachment*, Routledge, (2018). Co-editor of the American Psychiatric Press' *Infant and Early Childhood Mental Health: Core Concepts in Clinical Practice*.

Robert I. Watson, Jr., Ph.D., Supervising Psychoanalyst, William Alanson White Institute; Faculty, Institute for Contemporary Psychotherapy; Adjunct Assistant Professor, Teachers College, Columbia University. Author of chapters and journal articles on a variety of topics in psychoanalysis.

Introduction

On intense involvement with sports

Irwin Hirsch, Ph.D.

Background

Part of this introduction and most of the chapters that follow, first appeared in a special issue of *Contemporary Psychoanalysis*,[1] devoted to the examination of, and effort to comprehend intense involvement in sports, both in our culture here in the U.S. and worldwide. Joined by Robert Watson, Phillip Blumberg and I have expanded this journal issue into book format. There are two dimensions to intense involvement in sports – engagement as a fan and as a participant and of course, they are not mutually exclusive. Though the articles in this volume address both, they are tilted toward the understanding of "fandom," since in many respects the psychology of participation seems more transparent and less complex.

My introduction will begin with my own personal confessions and descriptions of a life, long lived as a fan of three sports. Though I have played and deeply enjoyed a range of sports between ages 9 through 70 and these were quite important to me; I was never especially accomplished nor gifted. I think that though most of us who are sports fans have also, to at least some degree, played the sports that capture our interest, this is not universally the case. Similarly, some who participate physically in sports do not become fans as well. The latter is most true with individual sports, like running, skiing and swimming. I believe that a background in playing team sports, because of the strong social element involved in these sports, lends itself to a sense of social affiliation to teams that are in the public eye, like professional and/or college teams. That is, there is a natural evolution from being a part of teams, even very loosely organized teams like with pick-up games in the schoolyard, gym or field, and being part of a fan base, all rooting for the same team.

Personal illustration

It's a cold night in January, 2009, a few hours past the end of an American professional football game between the New York Giants and the Philadelphia Eagles. The game I refer to was a playoff game between two of the premier teams competing for the world championship – The Super Bowl. I had been experiencing symptoms of depression since the last quarter of the game when it was obvious that my home team was about to lose. Last year they had won the Super Bowl, and this included winning four consecutive such playoff games. After each victory I was elated, a feeling which can be called mildly manic. Such mood shifts have been familiar to me since childhood, and are pegged not only to important championship series, but to virtually each and every game of what is now a 16-game professional football season. Furthermore, I respond in a similar but modified way to each of the 162 games of the major league baseball season, and to the 82 games of the professional basketball season. When my home teams win I always feel somewhat of an up and when they lose I always feel a corresponding down. Of course, if any of my favorite teams get on the road to the championship, these wins or losses affect me more strongly, and the high or the low lasts longer.

Why does using technical terms like depression and mania seem so accurate in this context? I do not become clinically depressed or manic – I am able to concentrate on my work and my relations with significant others are fundamentally unaffected past the very short-term. I use the term, "depression" to refer to a relative sense of gloom and pessimism about a wide range of things, a decline in energy and more than normal fatigue, and the inclination to brood and to ruminate. I speak of "mania" as referring characterizing an increase in energy and alertness, the wish to be socially engaged and, as well, a surge of optimism toward a variety of matters. I always imagined that I would grow out of reacting so seriously to these wins or losses (I feel silly writing about this in a scholarly venue, especially among those readers who are not serious sports fans; this is why I use the term, confession), though I have never really wanted my interest in these sports to wane. My involvement, since age 9 is reflective of a genuine interest – I read the sports section of the daily newspapers before any other section in the morning, scroll the internet sports apps, listen to sports radio shows in idle moments (e.g., shaving, driving in my car), and frequently discuss sports with men (almost exclusively men) whose interest and knowledge parallel my own. Some of these men are very well educated and may be characterized as intellectuals, and others have little education, though speak intelligently about sports matters. And some of these men are close friends while others are barely acquaintances, like countermen in food shops or service people whose paths I cross regularly or irregularly. I here admit to sometimes talking about sports with my patients who are also very interested and knowledgeable about this subject. Usually, I attempt to analyze the transference impact of these conversations, though not always. Many of my personal friendships and warm acquaintanceships, from childhood forward, began with a shared interest in playing and/or following sports. Sports is a major focus of conversation between me and my adult son and as well, my 2 grandsons, ages 12 and 13. I am especially thrilled that my grandsons are interested in these conversations and I cherish this connection with them.[2] The social richness of all of these relationships with strangers and intimates, more than compensates for the ruminative depressions I regularly suffer when my favored teams lose.

This said, I sometimes do consider it unfortunate that I have not grown out of my mood being dependent to some degree on the ups and downs of my beloved football, baseball and basketball teams – a sign of immaturity perhaps. Even when there is little to love about these teams I react affectively, to varying degrees, to wins and to losses. Still, at age 79, I might go to sleep not knowing the outcome of a particular late night game, and when I hear the score upon awakening in the morning my day may start with a sense of gloom and pessimism or an energetic optimism. This is obviously not all that impacts my approaching day, but very often my mood is distinctly influenced by these reported wins or losses. As noted, this sometimes feels like a reflection of my immaturity and I frequently have wished, since even early adulthood, that I could enjoy this involvement without my mood becoming so regularly impacted. This is so, if for no other reason, it is extraordinarily difficult to win a world championship, and by definition, over time, sorrow inevitably occurs well more often than exhilaration.

I am, however, not certain that the level of involvement and interest that I feel can be truly independent of the consequences of winning and losing, and the meaning this has for me and others who consider themselves avid fans of team sports. Indeed, in light of the importance of involvement with loved ones, career, health issues and life and death world events, why should outcomes of games played between men who are strangers and who play for money, assume emotional significance? I suggest briefly, some possible answers to this question.

Sports fandom is often an intense distraction that frequently removes one from the anxieties, pains and difficulties of daily living. The affective reactions that I and so many others have to winning and losing games may both mirror and mask the elation and the sadness accompanying far more obviously significant life events. Again, speaking personally, when I am gloomy and/or ruminative about any number of important matters in my life, watching one of my favorite teams' televised games can help me forget these and essentially transfer my affective state to the game that I am following. In effect, the game becomes more important than the slings and arrows of my life. And, when the game ends and if my team loses, I then often feel more badly about this than I had about far more significant matters. My ruminations may shift to events in the game that led to the loss, dwelling on what might have been a win if only, for example, the shortstop had caught the ball or the quarterback had not fumbled. For a limited period of time these pains help mask my more serious pain. Alternatively, if my team wins, the high that I can feel masks and replaces my dysphoria. The victory of my team becomes my victory and I may not feel the vulnerability of a more personal sense of weakness, loss or anxiety.

Most would agree that strong interests and hobbies make life more rich and, as well, help as a distraction from the inherent problems and anxieties that are inevitable in any lived life. What

I believe may be unique about intense interest in sports is the added element of winning or losing. In this context, in addition to the value of strong involvement in something outside of oneself, there exists the impact on mood. With victories, mood goes up and losses may temporarily replace and distract us from far more important losses, worries and failures. Some may argue that this mirrors addiction. I would say otherwise on two counts: One can argue that passionate interest in anything constitutes addiction, though this is rarely or never argued in relation to art, music literature, woodworking, etc. The term *addiction* is only warranted when an intense involvement takes over and interferes with the responsibilities necessary for optimal living. I have seen this only when interest in sports devolves into compulsive gambling.

As must be evident, I argue that distraction, up to a point is essentially a constructive thing. One can engage the serious matters of living only so much without this turning toward dysphoria. Even in the most impoverished and war-torn third world countries, passionate interest in sports often serves both as an opportunity for exciting pleasure and optimism, and a unifying force. We, in the United States, are fortunate to have many opportunities for constructive distraction. In many other parts of the world sports is one of the few constructive escapes from the severe and often traumatic slings and arrows.

Closely aligned and inseparable from the intense pursuit of an interest that invariably impacts mood, is the matter of identification. That is, unless one feels a sense of identification with a particular passion, it is unlikely that distracting highs and lows will become a normal part of that passionate interest. In a reference that I cannot find, the comedian, Jerry Seinfeld, himself a devoted sports fan, remarked that, "we root for shirts."[3] What he was referring to, of course, are the colors and the uniforms worn by all teams. What I consider as this rather profound point is that passionate fans of sports will persist in rooting for their teams independent of the particular athletes who play for any given team. That is, the players who play for each team change somewhat from year to year and change entirely from era to era. Regardless of whether we actually like the particular players of the moment on our favorite team, we are still likely to root with intensity for that team. Ergo, we root for shirts and, indeed, we care about these shirts because we have become identified with them.

It is very common for fans, when dressing casually or recreationally, to wear their team logos on hats, shirts or sweatshirts. This is almost as true for adults as it is for children. The clothing characterizes a sense of identification, both a feeling and a social communication that a particular team is *my* team – I am part of this team. One may, in a sports related social conversation, characterize themselves as a "Yankee fan," a "Met fan," implying that this is element of an important identification. In this context, when my team wins, I win and when they lose, I lose. If my team is having a successful year, I too am a winner and of course, the obverse is true. At games or watching games in public places like sports bars, one can hear chants like, e.g., "We're number 1." That is, *we* win or *we* lose. Among serious fans it is unusual to talk of their team as a *they*. I dare to speculate that fans sometimes feel worse about their team losing a particular regular season game than do some of the actual players.

One might think that adults who live relatively rich and productive lives and who have multiple sources of important satisfactions and achievements would find the success of their team to be less emotionally relevant than those fans whose lives are more dreary or impoverished. Counter-intuitively, I do not believe this is so. I do believe that the power of identification is so strong that it transcends socioeconomic and racial divides. Fandom is a great equalizer – the wealthy and the poor, the educated and the uneducated, the Black and the White are all part of the same team – a *we* who wear the same hats and shirts and who cheer and despair as a unit.

The affiliations and identifications described above often create a sense of community, of belonging, of being less isolated in family, job, geography. The longing to be a part of something bigger has much to do with religious affiliation and political affiliation. Sports fandom provides an additional community, both for those who feel connected to other communities and those who feel the absence of affiliation. In our contemporary political world we often hear the terms, "nationalism" and "tribalism." These terms do not have good connotation, they are terms that reflect "us" against "them," "good" against "bad." They reflect sentiments that lead to hatred, even to literal violence and at the extreme, war. Though sports fans very often speak of "hating" their rival teams and use phrases like, "*I hope we kill them*," I suggest that this is, for the most part, a relatively benign form of tribalism or nationalism. I acknowledge that these words and the feelings behind them are very ugly and except in rare instances (at least in the USA) when violence does break out among rival fans, I argue that such words ought not be taken literally and that they should be forgiven, as a statement of affiliation and as part of a sense of competition. Those who are not intense sports fans probably find this argument morally weak and a sanctioning of violent tribal feelings. To this I would say that violent feelings and hateful sentiments exist in all of us and that "killing" our opponent on the "battlefield" of competitive sports is a fundamentally benign expression of universal affective states, as long as no one literally conspires to physically injure the *other*. I also note that these violent words of competition exist in the stands and on the playing fields of countries that are both capitalistic and socialistic. In sum, as a devoted fan of three competitive sports, I believe that the net value of belonging to a community normally outweighs the ugly words and sentiments expressed toward rival communities.

As noted earlier, I have less to say about participation in sports than I do about fandom, since the benefits of literally being part of a team and the sense of identification, community affiliation and social experience all seem obvious. However, a couple of the articles in this volume address individual sports, running in particular. One element that cuts across participation in team and individual sports participation is the value of commitment to an activity and for striving for excellence. In this regard, involvement as an athlete, at whatever level, is not very different than involvement in one's career or one's love life. The satisfaction of intense involvement and doing the best that one can do registers as an assent in any context of life. In this respect, the value of activity over passivity and the feeling of wellbeing produced by the former, links sports with pretty much everything else in life.

In conclusion, most of us who are intensely involved with sports either as fans or participants, experience this involvement as a source of richness. The articles in this volume make this very clear. Those readers who share this interest will likely resonate with the sentiments expressed in this volume and those who do not, might grow to better understand some reasons why intense involvement is sports is so important to citizens of the world across national borders.

Notes

1 Hirsch, I. and Blumberg, P. (Eds.) (2010). Intense involvement with sports. *Contemporary Psychoanalysis*, 46: 475–588.
2 When both my son and my daughter were growing up, the teams that they played on became more important to me than the professional teams that I adored since childhood. All through middle to high school I attended almost every game they played and my moods were affected far more than they were with the ups and downs of those professional teams. Indeed, I was not only strongly affected by their wins and losses, but with how well they played. At this moment in life I go to every athletic event I possibly can to watch both my grandsons and two granddaughters engage. And once again, my moods are dramatically impacted by their wins and losses and how well they performed. I am emotionally impacted far more about my children's performances than I ever was my own, in all the years I participated in sports.
3 One of the truly great loves of my life between ages 10–17 was the Brooklyn Dodgers. I worshiped many of the players and lived and died by their victories and defeats. I adored their colors ("Dodger blue") and their uniforms. Their departure in 1957 for Los Angeles was devastating for me. I still rooted for them until their replacement, the New York Mets, began their franchise. To this day, however, when my Mets play the LA Dodgers and I look at the latters' uniforms, exactly the same except for "LA" replacing "B" on their hats, it is hard to not favor the team who abandoned me. I still love their logo and their colors and their name, *Dodgers*. On a deeply visceral level my childhood identification exists, and exists powerfully, in spite of cheering for the Mets. However, to wit, the hat that I wear most days of the year is not the one that says "NY," but the one that says "B."

Psychoanalytic perspectives on intense involvement in sports

Chapter 1

Baseball's bisexuality[1]

Adrienne Harris, Ph.D.

This chapter is part psychoanalysis, part social theory, part feminism, and part autobiography. It is an attempt to look, very locally, at the production and interpenetration of gender in cultural and intrapsychic life, specifically, in the experience of watching and following baseball. To write this chapter, I had to remember and think about a lot of my history, but also about the history of how sports function in and comment on social life and culture. At this point, 20 years after I began to work on this project, how I think about "Women, Baseball, and Words," (my original title) is the outcome of my history with psychoanalytic feminism, and with gender studies, and gender theory. But this chapter is also an outcome of my history as a daughter, as a wife, as a buddy, and most recently as a grandmother, somehow always someone rooted and vitalized in the intense pleasures of baseball. Only recently have I had a psychoanalytic language to think about the pleasures of baseball fandom and the experience of looking at and being at a baseball game. To my surprise, the language comes from the Hungarian émigré analyst Michael Balint, who brought much of Ferenczian thought to London in the 1930s.

Balint (1959) took a wonderful journey to teach his readers about two key concepts in his theories of regression and primitive object relations. *Philobats* and *ocnophils* constitute two distinct types, or perhaps two modes, of functioning. Philobats seek stimulation and love the energy and motion of flight and action (directly or vicariously). The sensible, perhaps more delicate, ocnophils luxuriate in clinging, in a sensual hold, in security, in sensory and acoustic baths. Baseball fans, one might say, integrate both these modes of being. But Balint had more to say about regression.

Balint illustrated these modes of relating, and also of fantasy, in a wonderful essay, "Funfares and Thrills." Here I apply his terminology and his taxonomies to sports, in particular to baseball, with its unique properties of timelessness and sensuality. Regarding the funfare, Balint identified three kinds of experiences, which are available to us through the social and individual experience of the funfare. These experiences define our pleasures, our internal representations, and our longings.

First is catering, the pleasure of eating, being fed, finding drinks and wonderful things to eat, which have to have, Balint suggested, two characteristics: sweetness and cheapness. These are perhaps different versions of characterizing excess or *jouissance*. The second kind of pleasure involves aggression and a variety of forms of violence: fantastical, actual, and vicarious. The third pleasure has to do with something that alters your state: dizziness, flight, the deliberate encounter of vertigo or giddiness. Linking these concepts to baseball, I found these concepts to be wonderful. There are the regressive pleasures of eating, watching, and, simultaneously, mimetically linking oneself to flight, to physical mastery, and to a multidimensional, multimedia experience of meaning and discourse as core aspects of watching and following baseball. In the very structure and experience of baseball, there are many features that make regression a particularly inspired idea to explore.

The first paper I wrote on this subject was very much embedded in the work of psychoanalytic and cultural feminism, which came into prominence in the 1980s, particularly Kristeva (1980, 1982) and Irigaray (1985, 1990). This perspective took an often monolithic view of gender and of patriarchy. It was a seemingly simple translation and reversal of Lacanian theory: language requires of its users a *position* in relation to desire and authority. Entering the world of language or acquiring speech constitutes subjectivity and genderedness for each individual. Not much space for bisexuality, for resistance, or for ambivalence.

In my initial ideas about baseball, women, and words, I was very much aware of baseball as a particular male space. I looked at several nested problems: How does baseball as a part of mass culture reflect and produce masculinist ideology? How do language and the intricate glossing practices through which baseball is interpreted ensure it as male preserve? How is baseball appropriated as male space? How—and why—are women kept out?

Baseball certainly has been situated primarily and historically as a male world. Moreover, it is a male world whose magic depends on the absence of women. Baseball is impenetrable by women. Women have been read out of baseball as subjective actors. Even having sued their way into locker rooms, having been drawn into major league status as part of the war effort, or having cajoled their way into the stands, women as subjects in baseball are marginal. Ann Ardour, a Toronto sportswriter traveling with the Toronto Blue Jays baseball team in the 1970s, remembers buckling her seat belt on an airplane while flying with the team and having a flight attendant lean over her to inquire, "Are you somebody's mother?" (personal communication).

If not someone's mother, she might have been somebody's daughter. For me, getting to baseball came through my father and as a way to find my father. I was taught to play baseball virtually the day after my father returned from the Second World War. There is a picture of me, dated August 1945. My father, standing behind me, has a catcher's mitt. I am wearing a red coat with a velvet collar. Batting left-handed, I am, as my father had instructed, leaning into the pitch. In the same era he and I went to see the International League games in Toronto in the 1940s and 50s, and, most deliciously, my father took me to the Polo Grounds to see Stan Musial play in a double header. The St. Louis Cardinals had been my father's team since his boyhood and Musial[2] his favorite modern player. There is a vague hint in this memory of trouble to come, as Musial, very unusually, went hitless in both games, and I left the Polo Grounds feeling inexplicably implicated in this disaster. But there were other gains. I have a personally autographed picture of Ducky Medwick.[3] From my husband's point of view, this is the really crucial part of my dowry. My father took no interest in my formal education, but had one requirement for a fully furnished mind: I should be acquainted with baseball, at least with its history for the 30 years prior to my birth. Dutifully, as a little girl, I immersed myself in back issues of *Baseball Register*, read books about the great teams of the 20s and 30s, and as a 13-year-old spent one summer writing and rewriting the opening paragraph of a novel

I intended to base on the 1919 Black Sox scandal,[4] a key line naturally being, "Say it ain't so."

For over a decade, in the 1980s, I lived on the edge of my husband's group of baseball buddies, a collection of men, many of them writers, who invented Rotisserie baseball.[5] They took me along to spring training and initiated me in an exhausting, engrossing attention to all the litter and minutiae of box scores. Every season could be a seamless experience of watching, attending, listening to, reading about, and talking baseball. Twenty-five years after these men had invented fantasy baseball, we all went to a "seminar" at the Baseball Hall of Fame in Cooperstown, New York, where a young writer gave a pitying analysis of the phenomenon of fantasy sports. He pointed out that the now grizzled guys who made up fantasy baseball somehow had contrived to make no money from it, despite having developed an enterprise whose ancillary income is now over a billion dollars a year. But even that horror could not quite evaporate the sweet moment of sitting in the Hall of Fame, being a part of baseball's strange and beauteous history. Inevitably, as the years rolled along, a patient appeared whose principal symptom was a serious addiction to fantasy baseball. So you can be someone's mother, someone's daughter, or someone's analyst.

But this entree to baseball through men captures the problem. If baseball is a social and material space appropriated by and for men, how can I speak? Or, if I speak, who am I? Clearly a tomboy voice and spirit is part of my baseball persona, but that sidesteps the question of a gendered, female voice.

When I began to work on this project, I thought it would be easy. But speaking from a position of love *and* disenfranchisement is a problem. Maybe, as an analyst, I should have known that. Writing about baseball immediately raises the problem of legitimacy and authority. A voice from the margins can be insightful and free, or that voice can be subversive. But it is often a voice tinged with envy, tortured with fear of being judged incompetent or inauthentic. To speak as a woman about baseball is to be immediately entangled in its discursive practices and in its ideological functions and to be at odds with its rules, its regulations, and its history.

When I gave a version of this chapter as a talk at Rutgers University in the 1980s, one of my graduate students, a man, said, with a rather pained look, that the talk was "interesting" (he seemed to use the word gingerly), but that really he didn't actually like to hear a woman speaking about baseball. The whole point of the game, the obsessions with the cards and the stats, is that these are perfect latency-stage devices, designed to exclude the sound of your mother's voice. The experience of hearing the talk had made him feel a little dizzy, perhaps even, he ventured, a little queasy.

However, a friend offers a different take on this matter of baseball and women. A serious and productive clergyman, with a lifetime of activism and social service behind him, he tells me quite simply that his adult life is still measured against his failure to play for the New York Yankees. For him, playing baseball was all about the hope of attracting the attention of a beautiful woman. I forbear mentioning Bernard Malamud's (1952) novel, *The Natural*. The woman in white, whose loving gaze you long for, can in another, angry, disappointed mood, shoot you. But, of course, these personal and literary examples of linking love of baseball to love of women doesn't actually help my problem. Loving or killing, the woman watches a man play baseball, and it is this structure's discursive tropes and conventions that I become tangled in.

Now, more than 20 years after I began this preoccupation with writing about baseball, I can see that this chapter has become an account of my own trajectory in psychoanalytic feminism. I began this work with an analysis of language and speech practices as exclusionary and an analysis of the difficulty women have in speaking as subjects. I was interested in the more general problematic of female desire and agency and felt indebted to Kristeva (1982) and the French feminist tradition influenced by Lacanian conceptions of the subject, language, and sexual difference.

I wrote myself into a *cul de sac*.

Now I can write myself out of that dead end through the more contesting systems of postmodern feminism, in particular Butler's (1997a, 1997b, 2005), as well as the work in culture studies in which the singular and monolithic power of patriarchy or ideology or male gaze is contested, a perspective in which hybridity and multiple points of enunciation are possible (Bhabha, 1994). My views now are more consistently psychoanalytic, in the sense that I view gender and its cultural constitution and maintenance as unstable, constructed scenes and sites. I see baseball now as a more fragile male space, more contested ground, more bisexual, and, in Balint's (1959) sense, more primitive and regressed. At this point in my thinking, I would stress the centrality in baseball of the preoedipal father/mother/parent as much as the oedipal scene in thinking about who inhabits baseball space. My argument is about sports in general and baseball in particular as elements in mass culture, implicated in and powerful in the individual's construction of self. This self may be national, gendered, or embodied. Baseball, as it is played but, most crucially, as it is narrated, is one cultural site for the structuring and elaborating of masculinity and American-ness. By deconstructing the argument, I claim that baseball is more accurately a site where gender is fragile and complex and potentially contestable.

Sports and ideology

There are many intriguing ways to think about sports in society and in psychic life, ideas that draw from psychoanalysis, from critical theory, and, in particular, Foucault (1966), who would see sports as a site or a spectacle in which key interests and power within a society create and maintain norms and cultural ideals.

Sports generally, and baseball in particular, are crucial elements in the construction of self, national or civic self, often presented in the guise of pure spectacle. The power of these structures and scenes to shape and constrain personhood and identity, both gendered and national identity, is often masked. C.L.R. James (1963) wrote a wonderful book on cricket, in the context of colonialism and British imperialism. He was a superb cricketer from Trinidad, a fact often trumped by his powerful career as a political theorist and Trotskyist in a period when that designation meant something interesting. He was fascinated by a national game stressing fair play, rules, and sportsmanship in a country from which he had direct evidence of that culture's history of exploitation and imperialism. Sports, fairness, amateurness is, in this guise, the perfect mask for capitalism, taming conflict into play. There has been very interesting writing on the Olympics in this regard (Brohm, 1978). The work of Harry Edwards (1973), the American sociologist, is another example of these ideological treatments of sports. In his critique of sports as a supposed path to upward mobility for poor, and particularly black, athletes and athletes of color, he argues that professional team sports create a gladiator class and considerable underdevelopment of large groups of second-tier athletes. College football supports the illusion of class mobility. But, as we now see, the onset of Parkinson's disease and dementia, as an aftermath to football careers, makes some sports writers think of football in the same spirit as dog fighting. Michael Vick[6] is the link to both settings.

Another argument maps the character of sports to the character of labor, particularly industrial labor. The public performance of a sport orchestrates management of impulse, a disciplining of the body, a theater for submission and masochism from which desire seems to have been almost drained. Most modern sports, at least in some aspects, are antipleasure, devoid of playfulness. The ravages done to the body and spirit by modern work can be masked if we take this assault and turn it into high art, and creative effort (Brohm, 1978).

In the 1996 Olympics, the spectacle of miniature young women gymnasts engaged in fracturing, splintering, and bruising their bodies while exhorted by elderly, violent, male coaches, on the side-lines, was a topic of great public debate. The spectacle, as child abuse and child labor law violation, was not lost on many. The positioning of women in that spectacle was quite remarkable. Official coaches of the team, both women, were reduced to caretaking, escorting functions while the media constructed the real psychodrama between the little mechanical girls, whose only powerful, authentic affect came with the horror of misstep and the bellowing and embracing men directing this spectacle from seats above it.

What is true of modern work, modern education, modern testing, and most modern sports is that they are all done to an increasingly speedy tempo. Many sports, like track, football, soccer, and basketball, position men against time as well as against each other. From the most grueling marathon to the split-second track event, athletes are held to the regulatory judgment of the clock, punitively calibrated to the millisecond. The athlete's body is held in an intense and masochistic relationship to the clock, a metaphor for technological machinery. Racing against the clock, fighting to the bell, playing out a last period, pits man against time with the implicit threat that the body can be broken in this struggle, depleted and wrecked in a battle with an implacable, relentless machine—time. We will see later how baseball, uniquely in modern North American sports, disrupts this facet of sports, particularly its masochism.

Because sporting experience is so much in the realm of spectacle and physical action, ways of being and looking are interpreted as normal and natural. So the constitutive and constructive aspects of baseball's work on masculinity become masked by the focus on natural talents and physical acumen. This is yet another ideological move, setting the ideals of the body and of play and fairness in the world of physical action. This strategy (which is both political and cultural) naturalizes, idealizes, and essentializes ways of being collective and ways of having a body.

An argument advanced by Cary Goodman (1979) would have it that Eros, playfulness, desire, and youth are removed from the social body through organized sports. His work examined the eradication of street games from the Lower East Side, an eradication he saw as the cooptation of immigrant energy and working-class spirit in the early years of the 20th century. Assimilation was in part accomplished by moving a sense of collectivity from the streets into the playgrounds, organized games, and sports leagues, arranged and maintained by bourgeois reformers and even the police (Police Athletic Leagues). Some of that type of critical analysis feels too behaviorist. It makes sports like prison, nothing but cooptation and management of body and desire. Perhaps we need to remember Balint's (1959) interest in the funfare as a site of vertigo and dizziness, as well as aggression. But also we need to be suspicious of what fun and play may be masking. In the production of modern sports activity—both at the amateur and at the professional level—many transfers are effected. The body is a site of transfer, and standards of normativity in matters of race, ethnicity, and class might be seen to be part of the powerful conflicts around baseball personnel from the 1940s onward.

Note how absolutely gender has been excluded from these evolutions of the baseball body.

There is the additional ideological operation through which ideas about the functioning of the state are subtly conveyed. The glorification of the "game," the taming of struggle into "fair competition," the very notion of "fairness" and rule-governed behavior in the context of lawless capital development and imperialism, all created a false vision of social life. Recall that the period of baseball's development overlaps and coincides with great movements of capitalism and industrialization from the late 19th century onward. Brohm (1978) evokes some of these questions of ideological and political masking in a startling insight in which he connects sports and social repression in the use of the soccer stadium in Chile as the site for mass torture and murder during the coup.

I am treating sports as a theatrical space for the display of bodies and bodies in motion. Inevitably gender is involved. As psychoanalysts, we could, it seems to me, be very interested in the creation, on a mass and public level, of highly elaborated fantasy material, which becomes available for the very stuff of intrapsychic life and subjectivity. Sports figures and their play are part of the social practices or social material through which the self is created and maintained at an individual and at a social level. Popular sports are part of the process through which male subjectivity is elaborated, and, in relation to masculinity, female objectivity is similarly installed.

Approaching sports from a more dynamic psychoanalytic perspective, we might see an arena of conflict and resistance in which the liberatory impulses still remain alive. There is in many athletic events (whether we watch or play) a longing to break through, to transcend, a fierce determination to be better, higher, stronger that speaks to the ineluctable aspect of human desire and against a simple notion of blind conditioning. This is what Balint (1959), I believe, was trying to conceptualize when he wrote of the experiences of vertigo at the funfare, that is, the impulse to fly free, to soar.

Psychoanalytic theory is written in as different and more subtle a register than the often mechanistic pitch in much of the standard forms of ideology critique. The control of individuals by the state is not a simple cause and effect. From Althusser (1971) onward, we are increasingly interested (influenced by psychoanalysis) in the forces of interpellation. Put in a simpler way, how does the state, the dominant culture, get us to *want* to do what we *have* to do? Sports provides an interesting way to answer that question. Approaching sports from a more dynamic perspective, we might see an area of conflict and resistance in which the liberatory impulses remain alive. In the race against the clock, there is masochism, but also desire, longing, and activity. There is, in many athletic events engaged in or watched, a longing to break through, to transcend, to step outside the quotidian or boundaried time and space. But, if we think dialectically, this potent feeling of transcendence systematically masks or disguises a lot of gamy economic realities: the ubiquity of gambling, the money that underwrites most so-called amateur sports, and so forth. But fairness and equality are ideals worth promoting. Utopian dreams may well be manipulated in public sports spectacles, but remain as potential, perhaps as dreams. These transcendent aspects of sports, and the powerful celebration of activity and, in some cases, collaborative play, always makes me feel acutely the loss to women of this cultural and social practice (as spectators and as players).

Baseball and time

Baseball specifically is unique as a social mirror. Baseball has its effects on us in unusual and idiosyncratic forms. First in its relation to time, and second in its relation to words and narratives, baseball works its magic on the psyche in specific ways. It is a spectacle certainly, a site of cultural practice, but more than most other sports, baseball is always interpreted, its narratives inseparable from its images and spectacles.

Baseball is a place without time, or, rather, a place preserved from measured metronomic temporality. Baseball is a place without women as agents. It provides men with the connected luxuries of no stopwatch, no schedule, and no women. Baseball also carries and maintains a false, made-up Disneyland history, a utopian vision of preindustrial America, idyllic, and problem free. It inhabits and produces an imaginary past. It is less obviously enmeshed than football or basketball in the economy of gambling, in the traffic of commerce. Baseball is more heavily symbolized, more drenched in liturgy than almost any other mass sport. It has a much tighter fit with art forms, novels, poetry, and narrative than do most other popular mass-audience sports.

One primary interpretive production is its birth myth, that is, the imaginary origins of baseball. The myth of baseball's beginnings is that it originated in a pretimed, preindustrial America, America before the stopwatch, that technological invention of industrial labor. Mythically, also, baseball evokes an America before feminism and suffrage. Baseball actually grew out of two social sites—gentlemen's athletic clubs and industrial teams. The industrial teams were probably a manipulative effort to counteract the impulse around union organizing by tapping the spirit of collectivity and loyalty for management, rather than collective bargaining. This exploitation of class solidarity by corporate owners, is, at the professional level, the transfer that Goodman (1979) noted in amateur youth sports, where human youthful energy was put to the use of regulation and body/mind management via organized sports such as the Police Athletic League. Now the link between baseball and corporate America is more revealed in the names of new minor and major league parks: Pacbell, Busch Stadium, Citi Field, and the like. Team names themselves still retain the preoccupations of latency boys: birds, animals, clothing: the Red Sox, the Cardinals, the Tigers, the Cubs, the White Sox.

During the baseball strike in 1981, a joke passed among baseball writers. When Lincoln was shot and lay dying, he summoned Abner Doubleday[7] to his bedside. "Don't let baseball die," he said. The joke masks a sanctified American fiction, the narrative of baseball's link to the heroes of the Civil War. The "national pastime" in this apocryphal story was thus invented by the victorious Civil War general, its virgin birth occurring in a perfectly pastoral village in upstate New York. Baseball is a game for lads after work, for gentlemen on the village green. This is its timeless birth image, the Hall of Fame at Cooperstown, its basilica.

Here is Roger Angell (1962), the main modern poet of baseball, describing being at a game: "The players below us—Mays, DiMaggio, Ruth, Snodgrass, swim and blur in memory, the ball floats over to Terry Turner and the end of this game may never come" (p. 303). We are in a world suspended, timeless. We are in an environment of lovely men, of movement and flight, of balls floating, men sliding. This is Balint's (1959) funfare. Competition, it seems, is less potent here. This is preoedipal life, as we see, as much potentially the province of women as of men, yet still lived as endless boyhood.

Baseball is a liturgical experience; its forms preserve and yet also construct historic memory, keeping alive a newly invented and reinvented timeless tradition. The foregoing quote was from the high priest writing in this religion, Roger Angell. A younger writer, W. P. Kinsella (1982) produced a short story, "Shoeless Joe Goes to Iowa," later a film called *Field of Dreams* (1989), in which a hero, patiently watched by a luscious wife (whose images in the novel virtually always involve food), builds an imaginary ballpark in a cornfield where he replays the crucial games in a futile evocation of lost desire and hope, a repetition before the trauma, the splitting of baseball's goodness, before the Black Sox scandal. The repair of that trauma involved the establishment of a commissioner, a benign but autocratic and omnipotent judge, in fact, a man whose earlier activities on the bench included the persecution of the early 20th century radicals.[8]

Baseball lives in an imaginary history, an endless present, always imbued with its own past. Baseball lives in a time warp without a second hand on the clock. It could get late, it could rain. Or it could get dark. Until very recently, one major league team played in a field with no lights, preserving the history of afternoon ball and its lyrical sunny setting. Baseball is radically different from other mass-consumer sports in its relation to time. It is both outside time and also continuous. You get two hits of football a week. Baseball is daily, hourly, weaving through one's day. Morning box scores, later editions for the West Coast games, afternoon TV. The radio chattering through the summer night air. There are also the endless secondary productions—books, cards, magazines, statistical analyses, editorials on the relation of baseball to life and manhood. And in the modern era, the Internet and a horde of bloggers keep baseball in an eternal present.

When the football strike threatened in the late 1980's, novelist Frederick Exely (1982) feared an upsurge in domestic violence in the absence of these hurtful struggles. Around the time of the baseball strike, different fears emerged. It was the loss of purity; the intrusion of money; worst of all, the intrusion of all the grit and clang of unions and labor struggles and economic and class conflict, the very social features baseball was organized to override and deny. It was (and Roger Angell (1978) related to the league expansions in the same way) a threatened loss of the past and therefore of identity, of the known constructed and seemingly "remembered" world of men's childhood. Pregenital, sublimated, phallic.

Baseball and words

Baseball is played and displayed in the mass media, but always it is glossed, interpreted, spoken. Familiar to relational or social constructivist analysts, baseball is a place where reality is constructed and made meaningful through narratives and discourse. So my thinking about baseball took me to words, writings, broadcasting, and linguistic practices as crucial elements in the production and internalization of baseball.

Baseball is talked as it is played or watched—color commentary by announcers, you sitting in the stands with a buddy, talking to a stranger sitting behind you, yelling. Baseball is all about words. Marbled through the visual jewel of baseball, its green geometry, its stately pacing, and its arcing, irregular movements, there is speech. Men talk when they do baseball. Unlike the tempo of hockey or basketball, where speech skates across the stream of continuous, timed play, baseball, because freed from the stopwatch, displays itself more amply and spaciously, opens large spaces and long moments into which words and fantasies can arch and curl. "Our afternoon slid by in a distraction of baseball and memory. I almost felt myself at some dreamlike doubleheader, merging the then and the now" (Angell, 1962, p. 302). It is impossible to experience this complex living in an endlessly present past and not think of Freud's (1914) meditation on remembering and repeating and the both regressive and narcissistic dreaminess of this experience, which Balint (1959), among others, so richly described. And to feel how seldom this collective and potentially healing experience exists, at the public level, for women.

In this endless moment of congealing memory, men talk. There is infield chatter; the laconic, reassuring voice of the old announcers; counterpointing and bitter remonstrance from fans. A sheet flaps down from the railing of a top deck, a hand-lettered love note to some player or team. Diamond Vision (the giant TV screen in most big baseball parks) writes and blinks on scores, and pitching changes all over the leagues. Each modality—electronic, visual, auditory, literary—has its own style and syntax, its own particular orthography or graphics or register. But all these dialects of baseball, these language worlds are in the male register.

Baseball talk has evolved as hip, low key, laid back, not too heavy handed or earnest. Nothing "bush," to use some old baseball slang (as in "bush league," the minor leagues). Now, that's a curious term to decode psychoanalytically. It indicates a mode of representation that is both marginalized and sexually charged. Baseball is the only literary domain I know of where the word nonchalant is used as a verb, as in "He nonchalanted it to first base," an apt description of a slow, but timely, throw to keep the batter from getting on base; an "easy" out. Sweetly, slowly, sensually timeless, and yet perfectly timed.

The style and talk of baseball writers is a ticket to the locker room and to the inside stories. Wilfred Sheed (1993), in an ambivalent review of sportswriter Red Smith's collected essays, complained, somewhat enviously, that Smith's material could only have come from a lifetime of hard drinking, hard-talking bouts with the guys, with the heavy demand to be able to keep your mind and wits clear, manage your drinks, and keep playing in the funny, jiving chatter of men talking sport.

I have on many occasions sat mute, envious, and wildly appreciative amidst my husband's baseball cronies. They are sportswriters, writers, and academics, but, more important, they are men lolling back in stadium seats or bleachers, who have been talking at and with and for other men, all their lives. Once, at spring training, at Al Lang Stadium in Florida, they all got press passes. I watched these same men move into the field and suddenly hang back, mute, adult postures changed into the slack, respectful body stance of eight-year-olds. I saw these men, now transformed into boys, as they watched beefy young 18-year-olds (those men, so "cruelly young," in Angell's (1978) phrase) take batting practice. Back in the stands, speech and adulthood returned to them, and they chatted and dissed players and each other. Al Lang Stadium—indeed many small Florida ballparks—are wonderful places to watch baseball as the March Florida sun hits the water behind the park. Someone has found a barbecue joint near the park and brings in boxes of ribs, beer, nachos dripping cheese, ice cream, the elements Balint (1959) so warmly evoked: cheap, tasty food. But, although the food and the cold beer fill our senses, the overwhelming impression I am left with is words, male words, and male wit, men's talk binding this afternoon together. Even the voices hawking food are male. I had no voice in this lyrical moment.

One could say that these men have the authority drawn from a lifetime with the stats, the lore, and the stuff of baseball. But talking is also a way of making authority, not merely drawing from it. The function of this talk is not only to make meaning, to gloss the game, but also to make self and self-in-relation. These words, the talking of baseball, bind men across generations and time, building up complex layers of experience, creating a thick piece of culture and ideology in which men act, coming into subjective and relational being.

> Baseball's time is seamless and invisible, a bubble within which players move at exactly the same pace and rhythm as their predecessors. This is the way the game was played in our youth, and in our father's youth and even back then, back in the country days—there must have been the same feeling, that time could be stopped.
> (Angell, 1962, p. 303)

Baseball talk comes in several registers, not just the heart-stopping prose of Angell. There is the ironic ear of Gilbert Sorrentino (1971):

> Telling you on the phone what Joe Chooch said about what Gil Hodges said down in St. Petersburg after Tommie Agee said something to somebody about something. So that was the final batting order, man. Your mouth open, what to say to him, Leo. Leo leave me alone. We are not friends anymore. Tell it to the marines. Tell it to Pete Hamill.
> (p. 127)

Phil Rizzutto, while announcing Yankee games, lived out some remnant of the games he played as a Yankee shortstop in the 1940s. He could go several innings with no mention of the game in progress. He talked about the difficulties getting to the game, the devotion to baseball. "I spend more time at Yankee stadium than I do in my own home," articulating perhaps the wish of many of his male listeners. He sent birthday greetings to cronies, chatted and squabbled with coannouncers, and occasionally commented on the game he was watching. These glossing practices brought the men who listened and watched into an intricate experience of themselves and other men at a game played over time and outside it.

Talk, banter, analysis, taunting, pontificating—all the work of baseball talk creates and distributes a complex, deeply connected male world. It is 1948. It is 1984. The man who speaks is a 28-year-old shortstop, a 60-year-old announcer. This voice over the airwaves, spooling out a million statistics and chatter and a whole background to all the players and teams, links Rizzutto and his listeners to a whole genealogy of men in baseball. The man listening connects to his eight-year-old self, falling asleep with a radio cupped to his ear, or to the 25-year-old pitcher warming up in the bullpen. This is an imaginative and imaginary experience of becoming an American male, made "real" in the matrix of words and images and action. The function of this talk, whether aural or written, is to bind men across generations, building up a thick layer of experience, creating a thick piece of culture, and embedding in it various matters of ideology and normativity—make that heteronormativity. This is the particular and special contribution baseball and its discourse makes to the reproduction of social life. Rereading this chapter now, I feel either that I am becoming the Margaret Mead of baseball, investigating hidden tribal rituals, or that I am the envious outsider, wanting in.

The pure form, the standard dialect of baseball, is a reedy, soft-timbered male voice, ambiguously adult, never harsh, and never seductive. It is a voice for the radio, for listening on a summer night as you drive home from the cottage or the beach. There is a story, perhaps apocryphal, that market researchers discovered that older fans preferred the radio as it was possible to assimilate the play-by-play to their imagination, remembering a game where all the players were white. The code for race is complex. There is a tough, black street style that has replaced the decorous, highly controlled, calm black voice of the Jackie Robinson era. There is Manny-talk,[9] perhaps outside the code. There are assorted versions of good-old-boy talk, Stengelese.[10] The sportscaster Red Barber spoke in a soft, androgynous, Southern voice. Each of the famous baseball announcers had a unique and recognizable cadence, until very recently almost exclusively male.

Dan Rosenheck (2004), a journalist with the *Economist*, wrote his senior thesis at Harvard on the representations of Latin masculinity in the major leagues. His title, "Hot Dogs, Hotheads and Hypochondriacs," speaks volumes. Looking both at the modern game, with its increasingly heavy Latin presence, and at the first Latin American baseball stars of the 1960s, Rosenheck finds, in a wide range of sports writing, the characterization of the Latin player as volatile, sensuous and lively. Masculinity is slipping, even as ethnic stereotyping is not.

Woman as witnessing object

I originally worked on this material from a Kristeva-esque, cultural feminist head. Briefly, what that approach permitted me to see was that the problem of a woman's entry into the experience of baseball was a version of her problem with relation to language: what is generally seen as a problem of authorship, of speaking as a subject. There is no female subject "I" in baseball, neither an authentic subject nor even the subject of enunciation since the language of baseball is so male coded. How to enter this both symbolic and imaginary space as a subject, a desiring subject?

To illustrate the problem, let me conjure up a historical figure (well known in Brooklyn Dodger lore). "Hilda"[11] is a famous Dodger fan of the 1950s, pictured often in news photos howling and shouting in Ebbets Field and passing notes to Leo Durocher, then the Dodgers' manager (and, coincidentally, another mad wordsmith). She is, in the iconic photos of the day, a woman with her mouth wide open, yelling, a figure of some anxious amusement, some contempt, even some irritation. Tough shouting is not a performance that can easily cross gender lines. Yet the biographical details of Hilda's life tell a particular story. She was an athlete turned into fan, one of those women, passionate about sports and, of course, disenfranchised and then subsequently rendered oddly, androgynously, outside gender.

But to continue the feminist trope on this problem of the feminine voice: a woman is a necessary actor but only, finally, as a mirror, a reactor. Women cannot enter baseball as actors, but they need to be near it as mirroring and admiring others. Theresa Wright looks supportively at Gary Cooper in the film, *Pride of the Yankees* (1942). Young women, packed into their jeans and cutoffs, hang out, leaning over the infield fences at spring training, waiting in the players' parking lot, waiting to be chosen. Women wait for men to be finished with play. I can be the *other* (necessary but marginalized), the "you" sent to the kitchen, the "you" standing in front of those flinty mirrors at Shea Stadium in New York, backcombing my hair, my head filled with fantasy. Susan Sarandon, in the film *Bull Durham* (1988), created the platonic form and ideal of Baseball Annie: mother, worshipper, groupie, one who knows in the service of male action, the perfect lover waiting for the season to begin.

If you don't want to enter as the object, you can as a woman enter as a kind of constructed boy, a tomboy—but being a tomboy is quite developmentally constrained, perhaps briefly, before adolescence, a last free space in which a female phallic style or sensibility is uncontested and unpathologized. You get a feeling for this restriction on the active female body in reading the commentary around female athletics from the early years of the 20th century and around the women's professional baseball leagues during the Second World War. As women began to do sports, at both an amateur and a professional level, many of the surrounding social concerns were couched in terms of gender appropriateness. As women's professional baseball teams developed, the concern was to maintain images of femininity. The chaperones and lessons were officially to uphold social priorities and to offset loose morals. The film, *A League of Their Own* (1992), which I always mistakenly misspeak as "A League of One's Own" (*pace* Virginia Woolf), appeared to stress the need to control female heterosexual desire, but the implicit worry was lesbianism and masculinity. Too often in the 30s and 40s, as these teams were developing both before and during the war, the anxiety was over some freakish androgyny. Joan Joyce, arguably the best woman softball pitcher and later a touring golf pro, struck out Ted Williams[12] four times in an exhibition. The operative word here is exhibition. Her skill was displayed as a sideshow, not legitimated. The name of the team of touring women players in the 1930s was Slapsie Maxie's Curvaceous Cuties. The Chicago baseball owner Charles Wrigley's wartime team was called the American Girls' League. Babe Dedrickson, a three-sport Olympian, was treated in the press first as a freak; there was a lot of worry over her androgynous appearance. When she married a wrestling promoter, the reconstruction of her image in the press was a stunning piece of gender conformity—the tomboy tamed. Her gigantic successes were matched by a giant husband, and often the couple were photographed or described in or near their giant bed.

Women, as in so much cultural space, cannot be fully subject in baseball. Siren or groupie, faithful wife or foolish fan, tomboy eunuch or androgen, woman as object is marginalized, locked hopelessly in the oscillating categories of good and bad girl. No "I" that can write or talk with comfort, no "I" in the right easy register, none of the dialect to produce and reproduce the social practices of baseball. And the problem heightens in my attempt to be a critic, writing a feminist critique of baseball and trying to make a connection between ideology, psychoanalysis and mass culture. A woman speaking about baseball sounds more than usually performative. A woman talking baseball could be a case of sour grapes or like somebody's mother telling the boys to stop fooling around, and forget all that phallic business with bats and balls. If the Rutgers graduate student I mentioned earlier is right, that is the hectoring female voice that sports was supposed to get boys away from. And, mostly bleakly, there is no way to speak with love; for a woman who loves baseball is too easily transformed into the one looking to be loved, into any of the varying forms of Baseball Annie, or as the one employing some odd, preoedipal strategy to be or stay the little boy, aka tomboy (Harris, 2005).

More complex social management strategies emerge when a woman owns (usually because she has inherited) a sports team. Georgianne Frontiere, who owned a football team, was pictured in popular magazines while taking exercise practice with the team and lying on the field with her legs spread. We get her imputed relation to the team. The other famous women owners are the Cincinnati Reds' Marge Schott, mostly disparaged in the press as eccentric, ill equipped for executive decision, and rather foolish. There is also Joan Payson, who owned and reputedly loved the Mets. Her era coincided with the tenure of Casey Stengel as the Mets' manager. Payson and Stengel appear in the narrative spaces of baseball rather like Margaret Dumont and Groucho Marx: ludicrous, comic figures. Payson's ownership of a baseball team was depicted as lovable, but silly, an old woman's slightly embarrassing fancy.

As an absolute requirement of maintaining its image and its ideological work, women are read out of baseball, excluded from its action and its discourse. Baseball is a gender performance by men for other men to watch and talk about. This was my gloomy conclusion 20 years ago when I began to write about baseball. Now I think of the problem with a slightly different spin. The shift in me is primarily due to the shift in feminist and postmodern thinking, in more complex models of identity (Bhabha, 1994; Butler, 1997b). I think of this linguistic, material, social world of baseball as a place where words and images and actions are coded in the male register and that women—as actors, as voyeurs, as scoptophilic agents—are problematized.

Postmodern gender theory and Baseball's bisexuality

I think, though, that baseball as male preserve is less secure and monolithic than I once did. I now think more psychoanalytically and more in terms of contemporary gender theory, particularly Judith Butler's (2005) ongoing work on gender and identification as performance.

All the descriptions of baseball—its timelessness, its rhythmic, leisured flow, its visual sensuality—could easily describe or metaphorize preoedipal, pregenital, polymorphously sensual and maternal and feminine experience. My husband' holds the memory of the smell of the grass as he first walked onto a big league field. My clergyman friend, the erstwhile Yankee hopeful, brings to mind the curve of the field like a large soft breast. Bart Giamatti[13] had a great idea about baseball: that it's the only game where you start from home and try as hard as possible to return. The nostalgia, the longing for a suspended past endlessly repeated—this is evocative of the thinking of Chasseguet Smirgel's (1985), of her work on the ego ideal and the longing for reunion. Regression within male space, or ungendered space, spaces like the ballpark, and like the funfare, are delicious sites of food and play and company. How interesting that this regression is coded as male preserve.

The baseball body also presents an interesting quandary in respect to masculine ideals. Baseball seems to me to lie in the domain of latency—its suspended sexuality, its sublimated energy with the time for calculation and preoccupation. Baseball imprints for most men somewhere between the ages of 7 and 12 years. Baseball's mythic heroes often have a boyish quality. Whatever the reality, there is the image of the childlike Babe Ruth, the polite, well-mannered, (now one sees) overcontrolled Jackie Robinson. There is a Boys Own annual aspect to these great players, the hard-pressing Thurman Munson (a scrappy New York Yankee in the 1970s), and his modern counterpart, Len Dykstra (nicknamed Nails), the proud and dignified Bob Gibson, an echo of Jackie Robinson, or the rapscallion Dean brothers, players of the 1940s. Whether hard-playing youth, earnest, serious schoolboy, or errant rascal, the screen of boyhood slips over these men. In the annual Baseball Register, each player listed among other things, his hobbies—that latency-loaded, atavistic term. Rusty Staub (an outfielder slugger for the Mets in the 1970s) was reported as favoring that ultimately old-fashioned boys' pastime, stamp collecting. He is, in fact a well-known and sophisticated wine collector and chef.

The body imago of the modern baseball player is probably one of the major sites of change. There is a more fetishized relation to the body and to injuries than in an earlier era. Sore arms are now rotator cuff injuries, and knees, shoulders, and other parts are tinkered with arthroscopically. Drugs, rehab, and confessions, as well as agents and corporate identities for the players, now dominate the media coverage of baseball. Handsome former players Lee Mazilli and Jim Palmer appeared in underwear ads. And on the contemporary scene, stellar Yankee players A-rod (Alex Rodriguez) and Derek Jeter both date models, actresses, and (historically) Madonna and now her contemporary equivalents. The more usual and traditional baseball body was considerably less sculpted, more old fashioned, less sexualized. Thurman Munson's (former Yankee catcher) nickname was the Pillsbury Doughboy. Two outstanding pitchers of the 1970s, Goose Gossage and Tommy John, men with mustaches, tobacco stains, and draped, baggy-kneed uniforms, looked like baseball players from the early years of the 20th century. There is none of the homoerotic and highly fetishized character of the football body.

Steroids changed much of this perception. Phallic power trumps delicacy and skill. Steroids and the MTV quality of large, modern, stadiums drown out some of this old vision of male space and male bodies. Michael Kimmelman (2009) looks with nostalgia (in its masculine form, let us note) at the great old ballparks. The quiet, the ivy, the absence of electronic spectacle: these are the particular and now unique features of Wrigley Field (Chicago) or Fenway Park (Boston). These parks seem like lost Edens. The steroid-riddled body, with its connotation of corruption, disease, and wreckage, links baseball to other sports: football, boxing, sports that exhaust the body as surely as any industrial machine would. This more digitalized, ad-driven MTV look to baseball may speak to the instability and anxiety in regard to the phallic ideal, even as these new forms of imagery shore up that ideal (Corbett, 2009).

If we follow contemporary gender theory and also trace what is always an impulse in psychoanalytic theory, we come to a view of gender as much less monolithic, more fragile, more tenuous, more constructed than in the standard psychoanalytic canon (Harris, 2005). In current terminology, gender is more performed than natural, even in baseball, that idealized essentially male sport. And since masculine gender ideals are built on repudiation and disavowal of the other feminine ideals, masculinity must be continually reasserted, maintained, reiterated, repaired, and replenished.

If we look at baseball in this light, its structures are ambiguous, easily contested. Baseball could be reread for its femininity, its androgyny, its evocation of regressed, luscious maternal space. If this sport is an important social site for the structuring of male identity, the gate keeping has to be fiercer. Baseball is probably a sport that could be integrated at all levels whereas tennis, football, and (except for goalkeeping) hockey cannot. Football is much more immune from femininity than baseball is, so the job of maintaining baseball as a male preserve is both more anxiety laden and more fragile. For this reason its language, and its narrative practices are more necessary than in other sports.

If we permit baseball's femininity to emerge, a much more complex structure comes into view, marbled with oedipal and preoedipal dimensions, potentially a place of postambivalence. My clergyman friend who speaks (seriously) of the green-mounded playing field as breast also reminds me of the astonishing effort and will of the player, the delight at display, the wish to be admired not by mother but by a contemporary girl. Hitting a major league fastball is the most difficult event of any sport. So prowess and energy and activity live in this sport, satisfying the philobat and the ocnophil. The desiring female subject in baseball has not fared so well as a site for identification with action and ambition. But the female desiring voyeur, hidden in the graffiti in the ladies room, is defiantly, even if politically incorrect from various points of view, an absent "presence." We might even hear in the howling fandom of Hilda Chester, the raging grief at the consignment to passive mirror, the longing of the mirror to spring into action (Golenbeck, 1984).

Baseball now has some women announcers. Bigendered voices and faces begin to be present, at least in some of the narrative spaces of baseball. Women apparently can talk about baseball. And I have insisted in this chapter on writing about baseball. Last summer, at the Staten Island Yankees' minor league ballpark, as

I was looking for french fries and some playground space for a four-year-old grandchild, I came across five or six Muslim women wearing head scarves and modest dress. On these scarves were perched Yankee caps. I wanted to weep and to shout with happiness.

Notes

1 An early version of this paper, "Woman, Baseball and Words," was published in Psychcritique, 1985, and reprinted in the Norton Guide to Literature, 1988. A later version was presented at the Oakland Skydome for the Psychoanalytic Institute of Northern California. Thanks to Sam Gerson, Charles Spezzano, Diane Elise, Peter Rutter, and Robert Sklar for their comments and support and to Donald Moss, who read an earlier version of this paper. And to my family, whose love of baseball was constitutive for me: George Harris, Robert Sklar, and now Jake Tentler. And to current psychoanalyst/baseball colleagues Stephen Seligman and Steven Cooper.
2 Stan Musial, a star for the St Louis Cardinals for over 20 years, retired in 1963. He was an all-round consummate player, with many baseball records in his time.
3 Joe Medwick was a famous player on the St. Louis Cardinals. He began his career in the 1930s, when the Cardinals were known as the Gas House gang.
4 The 1919 scandal in which the White Sox fixed the World Series and were renamed the Black Sox by the press of that era is one of the totemic moments in baseball. The purified national pastime was spoiled with corruption and gambling. It was a moment when the ideological impact of sport was threatened, its mythic work undermined.
5 Rotisserie baseball, the Ur-version of fantasy baseball, was the collective invention of this group of men around 1980. See Walker (2007) for the history and the evolution of this phenomenon.
6 Michael Vick, a star quarterback for the Atlanta Falcons, served an 18-month prison sentence for his role in a dog fighting ring. It is interesting that there is a universal horror at dog fighting but a billion dollar industry in professional football and, in an earlier era, boxing, although these two sports are now widely understood as inducing major brain trauma and injury in the sports' participants. The best modern voice undertaking this kind of analysis is Dave Zirin, whose blog is a must read.
7 This figure, a Civil War general (1819–1893) was named the father of baseball, again part of the mythologizing apparatus. There is no evidence for his part in inventing baseball, but some inventor of heroic status in America was required.
8 This first commissioner, W.K.M Landis, son of a Civil War surgeon, was august and conservative. He purified baseball after the 1919 scandal, but he also kept it white.
9 Manny Ramirez, while playing for the Boston Red Sox, was known for bizarre locutions, drifty play, and what seemed like a genuinely dope-addled speech

style, leading to the sportwriters' coded description in many sentences beginning or ending with the phrase, "Manny being Manny."
10 Casey Stengel, the Yankee manager known for much tough talk and mangled grammar, added to the myth of good old boys, codgers as the wise geniuses of the game.
11 The most famous Dodger fan—perhaps the most famous fan in baseball history—was Hilda Chester, a plump, pink-faced woman with a mop of stringy gray hair (so she is described in her Wikipedia note). Hilda began her 30-year love affair with the Dodgers in the 1920s. She had been a softball star as a kid, or so she said, and she once told a reporter that her dream was to play in the big leagues or to start a softball league for women. Thwarted as an athlete, she turned to rooting.
12 Williams is arguably one of the greatest hitters in the game, and also a war hero, a veteran, carrying the wonderful nickname, by virtue of his slender frame, the Splendid Splinter. Striking out Williams has almost the status of one of the Hercules myths, the slaying of a giant.
13 Bart Giamatti, a former president of Yale, was the Commissioner of Baseball in the 1980s.

References

A League of Their Own (1992), dir. P. Marshall. US: Columbia Pictures.
Althusser, L. (1971), *Lenin, Philosophy and Other Essays*. London: Monthly Review Press.
Angell, R. (1962), *The Summer Game*. Lincoln: University of Nebraska Press.
Angell, R. (1978), *Five Seasons, a Baseball Companion*. New York: Popular Library.
Balint, M. (1959), *Thrills and Regressions*. London: Maresfield Press.
Bhabha, H. (1994), *Location of Culture*. New York: Routledge.
Brohm, J.M. (1978), *The Prisoner of Measured Time*. London: Ink Links.
Bull Durham (1988), dir. R. Shelton. US: Mount.
Butler, J. (1997a), *Excitable Speech*. New York: Routledge.
Butler, J. (1997b), *The Psychic Life of Power: Theories of Subjection*. Palo Alto, CA: Stanford University Press.
Butler, J. (2005), *Giving an Account of Oneself*. New York: Fordham University Press.
Chassequet-Smirgel, J. (1985), *The Ego Ideal: A Psychoanalytic Essay on the Malady of the Ideal*. New York: Norton.
Corbett, K. (2009), *Boyhoods*. New Haven, CT: Yale University Press.
Edwards, H. (1973), *The Sociology of Sports*. New York: Dorey Press.
Exely, F. (1982), Just who is 'the game' in professional football? *New York Times*, August, 22, Section 5, page 2.
Field of Dreams (1989), dir. P.A. Robinson. US: Universal Pictures.

Foucault, M. (1966), *The Order of Things: An Archeology of the Human Sciences*. Paris: Galllimard.
Freud, S. (1914), Remembering, repeating and working-through (Further recommendations on the technique of psycho-analysis). *Standard Edition*, 12:145–156. London: Hogarth Press, 1958.
Golenbeck, P. (1984), *Bums: An Oral History of the Brooklyn Dodgers*. New York: G.P. Putnam's Sons.
Goodman, C. (1979), *Choosing Sides*. New York: Schocken Books.
Harris, A. (2005), *Gender as Soft Assembly*. Hillsdale, NJ: Analytic Press.
Irigaray, L. (1985), *The Speculum of the Other Woman*. Ithaca, NY: Cornell University Press.
Irigaray, L. (1990), This sex which is not one. In: *Essential Papers on the Psychology of Women: Essential Papers in Psychoanalysis*, ed. C. Zanardi. New York: New York University Press, pp. 344–351.
James, C.L.R. (1963), *Beyond a Boundary*. London: Stanley Paul.
Kimmelman, M. (2009), At the bad new ball parks. *New York Review of Books*, November 19, 56 (18).
Kinsella, W. (1982), *Shoeless Joe*. New York: Houghton Mifflin.
Kristeva, J. (1980), *Desire in Language*. New York: Columbia University Press.
Kristeva, J. (1982), *Powers of Horror: An Essay on Abjection*. New York: Columbia University Press.
Malamud, B. (1952), *The Natural*. New York: Farrar, Straus & Giroux.
Pride of the Yankees (1942), dir. S. Wood. US: Samuel Goldwyn.
Rosenheck, D. (2004), Hot dogs, hotheads and hypochondriacs: representations of Latin masculinity in Major League baseball. Unpub. doctoral dis., Harvard University.
Sheed, W. (1993), *My Life as a Fan*. New York: Simon & Schuster.
Sorrentino, G. (1971), *Imaginative Qualities of Actual Things*. New York: Pantheon.
Walker, S. (2007), *Fantasyland*. New York: Penguin Books California.

Chapter 2

Some reflections on the romance and degradation of sports
Watching and metawatching in the changing transitional space of sport

Steven Cooper, Ph.D.

There is a frequently told story about humility, or what passes for humility, that goes like this: During a Sabbath service, a rabbi is seized by a sudden wave of guilt, prostrates himself, and cries out, "God, before you I am nothing." The cantor is so moved by this demonstration of piety that he throws himself to the floor beside the rabbi and cries, "God, before you I am nothing!" Watching this scene unfold from his seat in the first row, the chairman of the synagogue's trustees jumps up, flops down in the aisle, and cries, "God, before you I am nothing!" The rabbi nudges the cantor and whispers, "So look who thinks he's nothing!"

Obviously, the joke plays on the hubris of humility and is a part of the joke that humans play on themselves and others in everyday life and in our unconscious minds. I am reminded of this humility whenever I see a professional baseball player rounding the bases after hitting a home run and pointing upward to acknowledge the help that he's received. In this moment of thanks and humility before God, the professional athlete also seems to believe that God has nothing better to do than to strengthen his hitting ability. Sports are a central individual and relational arena for the constant interplay of hubris and humility. We push ourselves to great achievements, hunger for accolades from others, and publicly surrender to the outcome of our efforts.

Here I reflect on some of the idealizing and devaluing elements of sports. As a lifelong, passionate baseball and basketball fan, I need to say that mine is a view of the underbelly of sports. I am not focusing on the enormously healthy and adaptive elements of sports or the opportunities for physical and intellectual play that sports afford. Sports are, when all is said and done, one of our most treasured transitional spaces. My favorite description of the transitional space of sports was stated by Roland Barthes (1960) in a magnificent essay on sport (this passage refers primarily to hockey):

> By its very power, this sport sustains a permanent threat of illegality; the game constantly risks being faster than consciousness and overwhelming it. There then occurs a kind of test of sport by the absurd: the sport scandal. This scandal occurs when men collapse the slender barrier separating the two combats: that of sport, that of life. Having lost all intermediary space, deprived of stake and rule alike, the players' combat ceases to be subject to the distance without which there can be no human society: once again a game becomes a conflict.
> (p. 63)

We all know that in the transitional space the object is both loved and mutilated. Here I examine some of the more destructive elements of our idealization and degradation of contemporary athletes that I think are illuminated by a psychoanalytic perspective.

Let us begin with the idea that, as observers of sports, we are engaging in a particular kind of position. Americans are watchers. The average American is said to watch six hours of television a day, not including our steadily increasing time on the Internet, which is another avenue for watching sports. The objects of our watching are becoming more and more distant from us, in Marshall McLuhan's (1964) terms, despite the ubiquity of television and the Internet. This watching can lead to something that David Foster Wallace (1990) refers to as "metawatching." We aren't only watching sports now, but we are commenting on our watching and commenting on our commenting. Perhaps this "metawatching" subset of what Wallace has termed metafiction—writing about observing ourselves as we write—also applies to our watching. Our current sports culture seems to involve sports-talking, sports-criticizing, sports-envy and sports-hating—elements of spectatorship that I call "spechating." In these activities we are becoming increasingly removed from the actual experience of observing and creating vicarious identifications with athletes. In a sense, the transitional space of sports is changing.

Grandiosity, idealization, and sports

We need to live with others. Just one small part of Freud's genius was to detail how impossible this struggle is over the course of a lifetime. Sport is a place where we are at least allowed to break through the veneer of our civilized selves for a moment in time. In the heat of the game, we are less likely to hide our irrational fantasies about the importance of the game's outcome as it reflects on the trajectory of each of our lives. Sports are the antidote to the existential awareness of our utter insignificance. As spectators, when everything is riding on whether an idealized athlete steals a base, hits a free throw, catches a pass, takes a pitch, and now, in the fusion of contemporary sports and capitalism, signs a contract, we can ignore the profoundly sad fact that none of it really matters. In sports, we are playfully confronting our insignificance, and paradoxically this realization is, in part, why the stakes are so high. Moreover, our culture's focus on money and materialistic pursuits also is a way of playing with our insignificance. It is not surprising, then, that in a fusion of sports and finance the sports pages are filled with contract terms, such as salary per year, signing bonuses, trading rights, incentive clauses, and the like. Soon sports pages will be an extension of the business section of newspapers and websites. Fantasies of unlimited material wealth and athletic achievement fuel both the fire of omnipotent fantasy and immortality.

One of my favorite examples of the expression of grandiosity through sports in everyday life can be found in what I have said during the many games of basketball that I've played. Over years of relatively mediocre athletic ability, particularly in basketball and tennis, I have noticed that, when I miss a shot, what sometimes follows is a kind of self-critical rant toward myself, usually silently but sometimes aloud. It might take the form of, "You idiot, how could you miss that shot?"

Over time I began to be annoyed by this type of self-flagellation coming both from me and from other mediocre athletes. I've wondered if it was directed toward the self or intended for others to hear. To be sure, there are more confident or less grandiose players who take it in stride when they miss a shot, but there is also a kind of acceptable, normative, unconsciously agreed upon level of self-reproach (a compromise or social compact) for many. The compromise is self-criticism, and it rests between the silent acceptance of disappointment or shame, on one hand, and, on the other, a clearly disproportionate level of grandiosity about one's ability.

The utterances of an imaginary player on the basketball court perpetuate a particular kind of fantasy—for either himself or as he wishes to present himself to others—that he really can make that shot and that it is more shocking for him to miss than to make the shot. Thus the symptomatic compromise also resides in a self-critical home between the fantasies of being better than he is versus his actual basketball proficiency (or lack of it). At the heart of this type of self-reproach is an unconsciously grandiose fantasy that I encounter frequently in clinical psychoanalysis and in the daily lives of people inside and outside sports. I have referred to this phenomenon as "the grandiosity of self-loathing" (Cooper, in press). Self-loathing and humility in sports often masquerade as less shameful ways of expressing grandiose fantasies.

Sports create the illusion that we "could play center field," to paraphrase John Fogerty (1985); or in the words of Loudon Wainwright (2001), "You found out after living with her, you're not the man that you never were." We are always creating scenarios in which we are the man or woman that we're not. Sports often enable the fantasy that we are someone else. For when a mediocre player makes an exceptional shot, someone might say, "That will keep you coming back." A player lives for those shots because they show him something that could have been, might have been, but that, more accurately, probably couldn't have actually been. Players are addicted not only to the pleasure that they take in that good shot but also to the fantasy that a good shot perpetuates. Sports allow men and perhaps women, too, a place for what Corbett (2009) has referred to as fantastic phallicism. We can briefly imagine bigness and prowess in a safe place. Some of the fantastic phallic phenomena that are emphasized in sports are also to be found in children's literature and contemporary television; for example, the television series *South Park* features four boys of different ethnicities and with different physical and personality characteristics. They are all estranged from and, for the most part, highly critical of each other for various aspects central to their person, such as being Jewish or overweight. In each episode the boys attempt something implicitly or explicitly grandiose. They strive for new heights and allow their imaginations free reign in their small Colorado mountain town. In each episode they are humbled—someone always seems to lose the game, as it were. Interestingly, in each episode during the first three years of the program, the same boy, Kenny, dies as a result of their often mischievous activities. For a number of seasons each episode would conclude with one of the characters exclaiming, "Oh my God, they killed Kenny!" Yet at the beginning of the next show Kenny was somehow revived and ready to join the boys in his hapless way in their next adventure. As in sports, each new game offered new opportunities for achievement, competition, and fantasies of greatness or fantastic phallicism.

A related phenomenon in sports occurs when someone takes time off because of either physical or narcissistic injury and then returns. It is not uncommon for such a person to resurrect notions of being better than he or she was before the layoff. In still another version, the person keeps trying new sports until his or her level of performance emerges and is disappointing, prompting another move to something new.

Like athletics, poker offers many opportunities for the resurrection of grandiose fantasy. Poker is an interesting game involving organized forms of playful deceit. Millions of men and women gather together in the evening with friends to outfox each other. The participants usually play for relatively small amounts of money relative to their net worth, but the stakes are emotionally high because unconsciously there are very high stakes at play. For a moment of shared illusion—a transitional space in which everything is on the line—there is an opportunity to win and to obliterate the other. The players, suspending disbelief with such phrases as, "I lost my shirt," play with the degradation and submission of losing in a safe way. Bluffing is a socialized form of lying, a culturally disavowed activity despite its frequency in human conduct (e.g., Hancock, 2009). In recent studies, lying in general has been found far more likely to occur by phone than in person. Poker, however, puts people face-to-face in circumstances in which lying is not only allowed but often rewarded. Aggression against—obliteration of— the other is encouraged: Game On. Sports and games allow adults to compete and be aggressive toward each other in a safe way. The process involves a kind of symbolic combat or attempted killing: "He made a killing" in poker; "He killed me in tennis," or "Our football team dominated [or got massacred]."

These games involve a suspension of disbelief on a number of different dimensions. We delude ourselves into thinking that the stakes are enormous. We relive parts of our youths in a consciously regressive context. We attribute strength and omnipotence to the victor and abject weakness to the defeated. We all need to suspend disbelief in one form or other, whether through sex, sports, games, fantasy, intellectual pursuits, art, or reverie. For many people, though, sports are a primary outlet for this suspension of disbelief and bring much satisfaction. In sport, we experience "life's fatal combat" (Barthes, 1960), but this combat is distanced from us by the spectacle. It is cleared of its most dangerous effects.

Part of the suspension of disbelief involves our conscious and unconscious effort to create a view of athletes as heroic. This legacy is likely related to the actual dependence of citizens on soldiers in war. The community is fundamentally dependent on protection and acts of heroism, and sustaining the heroic myth helps to perpetuate a sense of protection. Sports is spectacle and, as Barthes (1960) illustrated so beautifully, serves the same social function that theater did for the ancient Greeks. One of the sources of power for sports, according to Barthes, is that it constantly threatens legality—through its power, the game risks being faster than consciousness and can overwhelm consciousness (basketball, hockey, and soccer are better examples of this potential for illegality than is baseball). So the hero is in a complex position in relation to the law—he upholds the citizenry through his creation of ideals, but there is always the threat that he will live outside the law through his feats and power.

Interestingly, sometimes in analysis, free association may be thought of by a patient as a form of sport. The patient takes delight in the knowledge that his mind will not remain still for scrutiny by the analyst, his consciousness threatening to out-speed his analyst's or his own ability to reflect on it. Although we do not usually think of analysis as "sport," it can be a source of pleasure and a venue for pushing ourselves, in self-reflection, in ways that we have scant opportunity to do with someone else as attentive as the analyst.

The hero also represents the ideals that we strive for in times of peace. The hero takes us out of our prosaic lives and creates an alternative culture for fantasy as well. He allows us to identify vicariously with him and to transcend our usual experiences and perceptions of ourselves. This capacity to identify vicariously with heroes is not unlike the way that many cultures (contemporary American culture is an example) revere children. We project onto children our hopes and fantasies for unlimited possibility and accord the children a great deal of freedom because of their innocence. Children, heroes, athletes, like the Greek gods, know not what they do. They occupy a place of omnipotence and, sometimes, the power not to live within the law.

The degradation of athletics: greed, devotion, disloyalty, and "spechating"

Given those predilections for idealization, it is not surprising that athletes are often in for a long fall from being loved to being envied, even to being hated. Our not holding on to a human connection with the athlete is, in some ways, expected. We cannot possibly sustain our levels of idealization because the idealization is predicated on fantasy. Poems such as Robert Pinsky's (1996) elegant poem about Sandy Koufax, "The Night Game," freeze these idealized versions of the athlete, memorialized in our minds when we were children. But the half-life of these idealizations for adults is far briefer.

Athletes exist in our culture to represent fantasies that are far more important to us than anything truly connected to who the athletes are as people. The athlete is a brand, not a person—Tiger Woods is sold on television ads at every turn. Many athletes are "looked up to" (another linguistic connection to their heroic and god-like status), and our collective dissociation or disavowal of knowledge about their vulnerabilities is denied. We deny their drug addiction, alcoholism, sexual misadventures, and use of performance-enhancing drugs. When we find out about their flaws, we often feel a secret guilty pleasure with their failures, and this pleasure may be related to the envy that exists alongside our idealization. In some sense, we also decry that they are not the transitional objects that we created. How dare they burst the bubble?

It is not by accident that some of our admired athletes get themselves into a great deal of trouble with the law and that the public knows about these infractions almost as soon as they are committed. Such revelations are not simply a function of the wider and quicker media publicity about crimes by athletes than are most crimes committed by ordinary citizens. Many professional athletes live in a kind of alternative universe in which drugs, weapons, and sex are constantly available to them. The temptations for living outside the law are ubiquitous, and it is not surprising that, being human, they succumb to these temptations. Many professional athletes also grew up surrounded by high levels of crime and their exposure to firing weapons began at an early age. As recently as 2006, Bob Hohler reported that a New England Patriots football receiver, Jabar Gaffney, had stated, "I would say that about 90% of players in the league have guns to protect themselves." In the same article, an NBA team official who requested anonymity stated that in the NBA, "I would say that the figure is closer to 100 percent than it is to fifty percent" (Hohler, 2006).

For the most part, athletes are relatively young, even younger than previous generations, when they begin their professional careers. In the National Basketball Association, in particular, more and more athletes were being drafted out of high school and in some instances skipping college altogether until 2005, when the NBA prohibited players from moving directly from high school to professional basketball teams. Young athletes encased in a narcissistic bubble of exaggerated accolades and pandering find themselves believing that the "usual" laws don't apply to them. The freedom and approbation that these athletes receive make them a likely target of admiration, envy, and hostility from those who live more prosaic existences.

What are the rules for athletes anyway? Their problems with drug use are more complex than simply the overwhelming availability of illegal substances. Steroids and other illegal performance-enhancing substances are not sought out by athletes in a moral vacuum. Part of the reason that professional organizations such as the Major League Baseball Commission were so lax regarding illegal use of steroids for so long (five strikes and you're out) is that it was in the best financial interest of baseball for athletes to have access to growth hormones and performance-enhancing drugs. While athletes are often vilified because drugs allow them to perform better and therefore receive larger contracts, more runs in baseball is also good business for baseball owners. In fact, attendance in baseball has increased vastly since home runs and runs in general increased over the last 20 years. The more a player's performance plays into our repository of infinite longings for possibility and identification with the player, the easier it is for owners to sell longings.

It is likely that sports fans and journalists have engaged in elements of dissociation and manic denial by allowing ourselves to turn away from the radically changing bodies and heightened performance statistics of athletes during the steroid era of baseball. The gratification that has accompanied records being broken has excited us in ways that has allowed us to be disconnected from rule-bending and frank rule violation. The sports industry, like Hollywood, relies on the selling of dreams. The more athletes resemble us in our daily life, the more difficult is the selling. One of the challenges for contemporary advertising using athletes is to try to valorize the ways that they live outside the law. For example, in some instances, shoe companies tried to exploit this outlaw, bad-boy status (e.g., professional basketball player, Allen Iverson).

Our interest in and admiration of sports have become degraded in ways that are similar to our attitudes toward romantic love and devotion. We love and hate athletes with passion, whimsy, and increasingly, disloyalty. We are fickle lovers who seek another as soon as we are disappointed. Devotion in the realm of sports has become devalued and increasingly almost nonexistent. It is simple-minded to blame athletes' acquisitiveness for money as the primary reason for the degradation of fan loyalty to athletes, a theme that is sometimes advanced in newspaper sports writing and sports radio programming. Although it is true that professional athletes are always seeking the best contract, owners and players alike collude in making it more the exception than the rule that a player stay on one team for his entire career. Owners are looking for the most successful athletes they can find and the greatest media markets they can exploit. Athletes are commodities to be bought and sold.

Athletes are not victims in this sports culture, although they are also not the only culprits.

Before 1970, white, highly successful businessmen essentially owned athletes competing in the National Football League, Major League Baseball, and National Basketball Association. With little control over their contracts, athletes had no say about where they were traded and had little power to negotiate their contracts in a market tightly controlled by the owners. In those times of so little negotiating power for athletes, it was common for players to remain in a more stable position on one team and it was easier for fans to feel a sense of loyalty and devotion to those players. Now, it is difficult for young people and older adults to feel loyal to players whose half-life on a particular team in any sport is relatively brief. Perhaps for contemporary fans more than ever, Vince Lombardi's aphorism about sports, "Winning isn't everything, it's the *only* thing," is a truism. Sports fans are becoming more accepting of players as serviceable pawns in a machine designed for winning. Teams have budgets; particularly teams in smaller cities outside major markets where budgetary concerns often require the dismantling of even highly successful teams.

It is striking that, in the last 15 years, teams that have won the World Series in baseball (Florida Marlins) and in football (New England Patriots) have let go of many of the key players who contributed to their success because they needed to reduce payrolls. The greed displayed by players in leaving a team to go for the best contract is the proximal cause for fans' disloyalty and ambivalent feelings toward athletes, but it is not necessarily the most important cause.

A particular culture of athlete-hating has been developed and cultivated in some sports radio outlets and sports sections of newspapers. In this culture, the athletic world is reduced to blame—an athlete's problems make him a "head case," or a player's going to a new team is reduced to, "He went for the money." AM sports radio (e.g., WEEI, which reaches the largest sports audience in the United States and presents the most listened to radio show from 7 to 9 in the morning) has become a huge phenomenon in the United States in the last 20 years. One attraction of sports-talk shows is the allure they hold for fans to engage in reverie at any hour of the day. They also have become an integral part of a culture that I call "spechating." The banter and dialogue on these programs are often quite contemptuous of athletes. The players are discussed in an objectified, dehumanized way. They are cattle to be moved around, branded, used, and discarded. In some ways, they are discussed, in Adorno's (1950) terms, as subhuman, other than human, which allows them to be degraded verbally. I am not pitying them, for athletes are among the most highly paid people in the world. I am, however, interested in how the spectacle of sports has been transformed into a vehicle for hatred of athletes. This particular kind of radio culture has promoted a kind of group contagion of degradation and hatred of the athlete that is hidden by the patina of a focus on their achievements.

Often the sports writing in newspapers is, of course, playing aggressively with the combativeness of sports. In some ways, the newspapers are criticizing with impunity, going all out in their own sport of spechating. At times they illustrate the irony of postmodern viewers—they are commenting on the sport, blaming and hating the athlete in question with impunity, and trying to tell us at some level that they know what they're doing. Sports commentaries often follow what has occurred in television-watching over the years—viewers have been trained to laugh at characters' put downs of one another, to view ridicule as both the mode of social intercourse and the ultimate art form (Wallace, 1990). Yet there is a level of dissociation in this form of contempt for athletes that seems to me different from the ways in which we engage in sport as transitional play. Part of the difference is that our activity as spectators who are cheering, booing, shaming, and admiring is not the same as it was in the past. We are not only viewing the athletic activity; we are also talking about the viewing and viewing the viewing at ever greater levels of abstraction. It can make "hating on the athlete" an easier, more dissociated experience than that of the ups-and-downs—the vicissitudes—of watching the athletes' accomplishments or failures.

I view the kind of hating of athletes that I am describing as not unlike the depersonifying experiences put forth in violent video games. It is not uncommon in baseball stadiums and NBA arenas to have loud rock music, bright colorful lights, a constant barrage of cheerleaders and various side acts that accompany the actual sporting event. We are being bombarded with a level of hyperstimulation that tells us that we are not just watching a game, we are being transported from our world of usual expectations of self and others. We are encouraged to express negativity toward opposing athletes; we are prompted by the sound systems in arenas and stadiums that play songs with aggressive content when our opponents shoot a free throw or come up to bat. The message seems to be, "Hate with impunity. Disconnect yourself from your usual expectations about good sportsmanship and courtesy toward others."

I don't view spechating as a universal phenomenon. Many spectators maintain levels of playfulness that never move into such extreme versions of splitting. Sports of all kinds allow the spectator a form of institutionalized splitting. For those of us who are capable of ambivalent feelings toward the same object, sports allow a place for the pleasurably regressive tendency to have good and bad guys on the athletic field. The culture of hatred in some sports media outlets cultivate spechating even if the sense of irony is never far away.

I think that we may now be in a transitional stage as spectators of sport. Athletes have fallen very far from their pedestals and are watched very closely by the media. The days of secrecy around an athlete's flaws or falls from grace (e.g., Mickey Mantle's severe alcoholism was never written about) are long gone. Franklin Roosevelt would no longer be able to direct photographers to focus on the upper part of his body to avoid featuring the effects of his polio. It is more and more difficult to create transitional space for sports. The interplay between the play of the game and the intrusion of reality has become more prominent. Many of our sports pages now relate to how contracts will be drawn up and who will be moved from one team to the next. We are also in a period in which the level of contempt and hatred for the athlete, driven primarily, I think, by envy, is also becoming intensified. Spechating has invaded the spectacle. It is creating a circumstance in which the love of sport, the admiration of the athlete's feats, and the playfulness of the lines between reality and fantasy in the spectacle are harder to sustain in professional sports.

Fortunately, this devaluation of athletes doesn't stand a chance in comparison with our admiration for their abilities and accomplishments. Our idealization of athletic ability also cannot compete with the elements of nostalgia that are contained in our admiration and appreciation of sports as we age. If we once enjoyed participating in sports, as did I, we are likely to recall our own athletic abilities and our own transcendent moments, no matter how average or mediocre our talents. In the reverie of nostalgia we long for home—the literal definition of nostalgia. We long for a time when play was our job and the suspension of disbelief in sports was a shorter jump from everyday life than are the responsibilities and stresses of adult life. Nostalgia and the recollection of our sports heroes and our own achievements allow us to dip back into that treasure chest of memory and, of course, fantasy. I remember with pleasure all the times, as I was growing up, I was at the free-throw line in the back of my house and shooting free throws that in my fantasy would win the game if I made them. The crowd was roaring and everything was on the line. It makes me long for the simplicity of the useless play of sport.

References

Adorno, T. (1950), *The Authoritarian Personality.* New York: Harper.
Barthes, R. (1960), *What Is Sport?* (trans. R. Howard). New Haven, CT: Yale University Press, 2007.
Cooper, S. (in press), The grandiosity of self-loathing: Transference–countertransference considerations. *International Journal of Psychoanalysis.*
Corbett, K. (2009), Boyhood femininity, gender identity disorder, masculine presuppositions, and the anxiety of regulation. *Psychoanalytic Dialogues,* 19:363–370.
Fogerty, J. (1985), Centerfield. *Creedence Clearwater Revival.* Warner Brothers.
Hancock, J. (2009), www.news.cornell.edu/stories/Nov06/SS.Hancock.html.
Hohler, B. (2006), Many athletes regard firearms as necessity. *Boston Globe,* November 10, p. 3.
McLuhan, M. (1964), *Understanding Media.* Cambridge, MA: MIT Press, 1994.

Pinsky, R. (1996), The night game. In: *The Figured Wheel: New and Collected Poems, 1966–1996*. New York: Farrar, Strauss & Giroux.
Wainwright III, L. (2001), *Living Alone*. Red House Records.
Wallace, D. (1990), *A Supposedly Fun Thing I'll Never Do Again: Essays and Arguments*. Boston, MA: Little, Brown.

Chapter 3

Revaluing sports

Don Greif, Ph.D.

Sports have played a huge role in my life—in my personal development and identity and as a source of meaning, pleasure, and fulfillment. I imagine this statement evoking a range of reactions in readers, including curiosity, surprise, and for some, mild disdain. For the sake of argument, let's assume there is at least a kernel of truth to this conjecture. If we assume that some analytic readers will feel a bit taken aback or put off knowing that sports have had an enormous impact on my life, let's ask why they might feel this way. Why would a fellow analyst's being passionate about sports not resonate with psychoanalytic readers, or at least be unremarkable?

I think of psychoanalysts and psychoanalytic therapists[1] as less athletic and less interested in sports than the average American. If I'm right, and not simply stereotyping, then many analysts, whose involvement in sports is less intense than my own, could well think it a bit strange, even suspect, that a colleague's development and identity were profoundly shaped by sports. Some might even think of this colleague as something other than a serious analyst.

The devaluation of sports[2]

I do not think that the less athletic bent of the average psychoanalyst fully explains that type of emotional response to another analyst affirming the importance of sports in his life. For attitudes of devaluation toward sports and athletes are not limited to analysts—nor to people uninvolved with sports—but are more pervasive, especially among well-educated, intellectual people, who sometimes devalue sports fans and athletes without even knowing they do it. This observation is based primarily, but not solely, on my personal impressions over many years.

People who are intensely involved with sports, including sports-obsessed fans, are viewed, often unconsciously, as philistines. Sports are thought of as less "serious" pursuits than, say, opera, theater, dance, or film. Unlike the arts, sports do not set out to address serious issues. Sports are seen—at least among "serious" people—as a form of light entertainment, a diversion or escape from the important issues of life. Justice Antonin Scalia reflected this view in his opinion in a Supreme Court case in which he rejected the idea that the Court "could determine the essential nature of golf." Scalia wrote, "[I]t is the very nature of a game to have no object except amusement (that's what distinguishes games from productive activity)" (PGA Tour v. Martin, 2001, in Sandel, 2009, p. 205).

Although there is respect for professional athletes' abilities and athletes are often adulated and glorified in our culture, well-educated professionals commonly see them—and others who make their living mainly through physical labor—as mentally inferior[3] and perceive what they do as relatively unimportant. Athletes may be lumped into the category "jocks," which is often preceded by the word "dumb." "Dumb jocks" may be the male equivalent of "dumb blondes," derogatory epithets that reduce a group of people to a lower realm. The denigration of physical labor, sports, athletes, and fans corresponds to a general devaluation of the physical, bodily realm of human experience in our culture. It also corresponds to a shift away from the Greek ideal of a sound mind and body, according to which a well-developed mind and a fit body were essential to be a complete human being. The Olympic Games began in Greece partly because the Greeks believed that organized games help the mind and body achieve equilibrium.

Sports and psychoanalysis

While preparing to write this piece, I reflected on the meaning and purpose of sports in my life. As I began to recognize the depth and intensity of my lifelong involvement in sports, I realized that I have a slight, but palpable, feeling of embarrassment. Moreover, I realized that, although I love and value sports, paradoxically, I also devalue those who are intensely involved in sports.

Simply put, I relegate sports to a lower realm than psychoanalysis, even though I am as passionate about sports as I am about psychoanalysis. I hasten to add that the two realms are indeed related for me, since one result of training at the William Alanson White Institute, especially of my personal analysis, is that I learned to be more playful and spontaneous—and have more fun—when doing treatment. Consequently I am much more effective as a therapist. Playfulness, fun, and spontaneity were qualities I always experienced, and took for granted, when playing sports; but I never knew they were "allowed" in the consulting room. Prior to my training, my approach to analytic therapy primarily involved rigor, discipline, restraint, empathy, and thoughtfulness. While it still has these characteristics, the "sportslike" qualities have been added to the mix. Parenthetically, my greater personal engagement with patients provided the crucial context for the emergence and integration of play, spontaneity, and humor into my therapeutic conduct.

It's also likely that my passion for playing—born partly of my having spent an enormous amount of my childhood and early adulthood playing—shaped my analytic sensibility and penchant for playfulness in my work. Conversely, psychoanalysis has enriched my athletic experience; my personal treatment has helped me perform better and I have become far more attuned to the vast mental dimension in sports. Therefore the relationship between sports and psychoanalysis has been reciprocally beneficial.

Sports and play

Sports essentially involve playing games. Playing games—all playing, for that matter—evokes images of children, since play is a central activity for children. In fact, it is often said that play is the work of children.

Conventional wisdom holds that mature adults outgrow, or shed, their passion for games and sports, which are viewed as remnants of childhood. Adults who are consumed or obsessed with sports must, therefore, have something wrong with them. Involvement in sports cannot possibly be as important as education, career, and family—can it?

Although adults who are consumed with sports may be considered immature, children's sports are often seen in many positive ways: they teach valuable life lessons; promote desirable qualities in children, such as discipline, determination, focus, and sportsmanship; provide healthy exercise; and enable parents and their children to connect. And sports can be viewed as an arena in which children can learn to handle emotions around winning and losing; feel comfortable and confident in their bodies; and acquire teamwork skills.

Failure and struggle in sports provide unique opportunities to grow. Teddy Kennedy, Jr., in his powerful eulogy for his father, Senator Edward Kennedy (2009), movingly described how his dad's strength and unwavering confidence had inspired him to sled—and provided a lesson for life—shortly after his leg had been amputated:

> When I was 12 years old, I was diagnosed with bone cancer. And a few months after I lost my leg, there was a heavy snowfall over my childhood home outside Washington DC. My father went to the garage to get the old Flexible Flyer and asked me if I wanted to go sledding down the steep driveway. I was trying to get used to my new artificial leg. The hill was covered with ice and snow, it wasn't easy for me to walk. And the hill was very slick. As I struggled to walk, I slipped and I fell on the ice. And I started to cry and I said, "I can't do this." I said, "I'll never be able to climb up that hill." And he lifted me up in his strong, gentle arms and said something I will never forget. He said, "I know you can do it. There is nothing that you can't do. We're going to climb that hill together, even if it takes us all day." Sure enough, he held me around my waist and we slowly made it to the top. And you know, at age 12 losing your leg pretty much seems like the end of the world. But as I climbed onto his back and we flew down the hill that day, I knew he was right. I knew I was going to be OK. You see, my father taught me that even our most profound losses are survivable, and that it is what we do with that loss, our ability to transform it into a positive event, that is one of my father's greatest lessons.

In spite of its many virtues, sports and other forms of play are still viewed as preparation for real life. Although Winnicott (1971) recognized the central role that play has for adults as well as for children, and ethological and brain studies suggest that "play may be as important to (human and animal) life as sleeping and dreaming" (Brown, 1994, p. 8), many psychoanalysts, reflecting widely held views, undervalue the vital importance of play for adults. It is not surprising, then, that sports have been relegated to a peripheral role in adulthood.

An alternative point of view is that adults who are intensely involved in sports—as participants or fans—are deeply engaged in play, an essential ingredient of psychological health for adults. Intense involvement in sports for adults, according to this viewpoint, represents a continuation of childhood play and a way to fulfill essential needs.

As is the case for children, playing sports and being a fan can meet many vital adult needs and desires: it can provide a common ground for communication, connection, and community; an arena to experience and express passionate feelings and competitive aggression; a place to learn to enjoy and value winning and bear the pain of losing; a place to confront anxiety and leave one's comfort zone; a respite from hardship and the quotidian; a source of pleasure and fun; an opportunity to be part of something larger than oneself; and a realm for grappling with, and mastering, personal challenges, inner struggles, and demons.

If play is an essential adult activity, sports can also be viewed as providing adults the opportunity to develop their capacities and learn to play, which, for many reasons, may have been stunted in childhood. Learning to play, as Winnicott (1971) elucidated, is a developmental achievement. It requires immersion in a transitional space between inner fantasy and external reality. Like art, it requires one to sustain the illusion of feeling that it matters deeply—and acting as if it were very real—yet knowing it is play and therefore not taking it too seriously. If it is taken too seriously, as Winnicott noted, one loses the ability to play.

If intense involvement in games or sports is to be psychologically valuable one must feel that it is very important but know that the results do not have ultimate significance Although I am referring here to optimal play, the "pathologies" of playing are rampant.

We know all too well the damage done by parents or coaches who act as if the results of games are life-or-death matters. We know, too, the potential harm done to children and adults by elevating or deifying winners and lavishing them with huge material rewards. The de-emphasis on competition and aggression has its own pitfalls and can be misguided if it is taken too far. In such a society, learning how to win graciously (feeling joyful and proud, and respectful of one's rival) and lose maturely (feeling bad but taking responsibility for one's mistakes without making excuses) is not easy. Learning how to win and lose is invaluable, though, for victories and defeats are normal, expectable experiences throughout life.

My experience in sports

My personal experience as an athlete and as a fan being the basis for much of what I have written so far, I would like to describe the role and function sports has played in my life.

While I was growing up, sports and games provided an invaluable way for me to express competitive aggression. The basketball court, baseball and football fields, ping-pong table, and golf course were places where I felt freer to express my competitive aggression than in any other place.

My father had trouble tolerating challenges to his authority, and my mother was easily injured, so I learned not to disagree or get angry. Instead I did my own thing under the radar and used sports as an outlet for expressing my competitiveness and aggressiveness. I discovered early on that I was very good at sports, and my older brother, also a good athlete, encouraged and helped me develop athletic skills as we played lots of games and sports together.

I wanted to do well in school and, when I got to high school, outperform my classmates. Yet, school was more private and less directly competitive than sports, which was direct, mano-a-mano, and more testosterone driven. When my father developed a major depression requiring hospitalization and ECT when I was 13 years old, sports were where I could express my competitive and aggressive feelings without (unconsciously) worrying that I might hurt him.

Because I was a natural athlete, sports also provided the opportunity for me to develop a strong sense of competence and confidence. I "specialized" in lacrosse, which I played in high school and college. I excelled in high school and as a college freshman, and my coaches expected me to go very far. For various reasons, however, I lost my passion for lacrosse as a sophomore and left the team. Had professional lacrosse existed (it was created years later but never attained much popularity, status, or financial rewards), I might have felt more enthusiastic about pursuing it further, but at the time I felt a little silly spending so much time and energy playing a kid's game when serious intellectual, existential and personal issues were engaging me more and more. Ultimately, though, my reasons for leaving lacrosse may have had as much to do with the loss of narcissistic gratification I had gotten from being a star in high school and as a college freshman. As a sophomore on the varsity, for the first time in many years I was not the starting crease attackman (the offense position I played). Moreover, the coach—with whom I felt little connection and for whom I had little affection—did not use me in the way I had been used for many years, that is, to score goals. Since I did not feel valued, supported, or encouraged—and hadn't had any therapy yet to help me understand what I felt without having to act on it—I quit the team, a decision I later regretted, mainly because I lost the chance to discover how good I could become at lacrosse.

The emotional power of sports

The "thrill of victory and the agony of defeat," the phrase made famous by the opening to *ABC's Wide World of Sports*, captures an essential emotional truth for athletes and fans alike.[4] When I played sports as a kid, whether it was one-on-one basketball, stickball, or whiffleball with friends, or team sports in high school or college, I felt the same shifts in mood—elation and dejection—that I do as a fan. As an adult, when I hit a great shot in golf, I am thrilled; when I have a great round of golf, I am in a very good mood for a couple of days.

Whether you're playing or watching them, intense involvement in sports can be mood altering and addictive. In high school and college, when I played well and scored goals, I felt excited and thrilled. I felt deeply pleased that I could do something that was really difficult and had taken me years to become adept at. The joy of execution, achieving a high level of athleticism, was the key ingredient and a powerful reward in itself. Sometimes, when I played exceptionally well—for example, when I scored six goals in one game in college—I felt an adrenaline rush that I would liken to a "peak" experience. When I was recognized for my lacrosse accomplishments with accolades and awards, I felt extremely validated and proud. It provided substantial narcissistic gratification, which might have been especially valuable because, for significant periods of my adolescence, I felt socially anxious and insecure, particularly with girls. In retrospect, I think sports was a vital source of self-esteem and bolstered my sense of masculinity.

Playing on a team and winning games and championships is unique. When my team won (90% of the time in high school), I felt great, and, if it was a close or important game, I felt elated. The shared joy of accomplishing it as a team—of doing it together—was powerful. When my team lost, especially if I had not performed well, I felt dejected. When my team lost and I had played well, it took some of the sting out of losing, but it still felt awful to lose.

For me as an adult, winning at sports feels far less important than it used to feel. Performing a sport very well, however, is still profoundly satisfying. I have gotten this feeling from softball and tennis, but mostly from golf, which has become a vital part of my life.

I recently rediscovered how satisfying and mentally challenging it is to perform a sport well under the pressure of formal competition. This past June I won the 2nd annual New York "City Parks Putting Challenge," which involved winning one of nine qualifying events held around the city and then winning a three-stage contest against the other sectional winners. The contest was held at Trump Towers; Donald Trump spoke at the opening ceremonies; a P.G.A. tour professional provided commentary about putting during the competition; and I was interviewed for a story on a Chinese television station.

Effective psychoanalytic treatment played a vital role in my victory. Because I had done enough analytic work on my personal demons, I felt entitled to win. Therefore, I was able to vigorously and strategically prepare for the contest and put myself in the best position to win. Moreover I maintained my composure under pressure because I could feel tense and anxious without trying to suppress, avoid, or deny it and was thus able, paradoxically, to establish distance from my nerves and focus only on putting. Of course, I'm a very good putter, but my point is that addressing my internal Achilles' heel enabled me to use my abilities fully. It is a truism in sports that, once you reach a certain level of technical proficiency, performing your best in competition is mostly a mental matter, which is why so many athletes work on their mental games. In my opinion, though, most athletes and sports psychologists pay insufficient attention to unconscious factors that sabotage performance.

Playing games and sports as a kid was so rich an experience that not to preserve it into adulthood was unthinkable. Yet, for short periods in my life I have been uninvolved in sports; these were times when I felt somewhat depressed. Only later, when I felt better, did I realize that something I loved—this mood-altering activity—was missing. Might there be something defensive about the fact that sports has been a key part of my identity and self-esteem? Of course, but the value sports has afforded far outweighs its defensive or protective functions. Hirsch and Blumberg ask if intense involvement in sports can be a "substitute for intense commitments to matters that are more intrinsically important" (2010, p. 478). and a defense against dealing adaptively with conflict and difficult feelings. Of course it can, but so, too, can intense involvement in any activity, including "serious" ones like psychoanalysis.

Is it possible that a *lack* of intense involvement in some form of play, sport, or physical activity can also be defensive? Might it, for example, protect some people from feeling anxious, insecure, or uncomfortable with their bodies? Might it protect some from the emotional dangers of playing and entering a transitional space? Perhaps one's capacity for intense involvement in sports reflects an ability to engage deeply in play. Perhaps, too, it reflects an ability to feel and care deeply about things. While sports may be a replacement for deep involvement in "more pivotal life events," we cannot know this is the case for anyone without knowing them very well.

I have experienced profound joy and despondency as a fan. When, at age nine, I went to the 1964 World Series and saw Mickey Mantle (my boyhood hero) hit a home run to win the game on the first pitch in the bottom of the 9th inning, it was one of the most exciting moments of my childhood. While Yankee fans came to expect dramatic home runs from Mantle, this one was electrifying. I still remember the roar of the crowd, the exultation, and the sense that all was right with the world—a comforting, perhaps useful, illusion. When Joe Namath led the heavy underdog NY Jets to defeat the Baltimore Colts in the 1969 Super Bowl, I (and surely thousands of others) had similar feelings. These experiences made me feel connected to, or merged with, a powerful force beyond myself, perhaps similar to certain religious or spiritual experiences. Maybe fan experiences like these simply make us feel important, special, or powerful, or perhaps, in some cases, they substitute for thwarted early merger experiences with caretakers; these explanations, though, while surely true for some, seem reductionistic. I think it's far more likely that such a widespread phenomenon is based on something hard-wired and integral to human nature (Pinker, 2002).

Sports: retaining connection with our primal nature

Ever since humans made the shift from hunter-gatherers to agrarian to industrial to postindustrial societies, we have become increasingly disconnected from our bodies and the natural world. As Paul Lippmann (2009) eloquently articulated, our connection to nature and ourselves may be more imperiled today than ever. Virtual, disembodied experience (computers, cell phones, PDA's), Lippmann noted, has gained ascendancy and replaced, to a large extent, embodied experience and contact with the natural world. In such a society intense involvement in sports and other bodily pursuits[5] may be a way for us continually to rediscover, recreate, and express a primal, instinctive, untamed or wild aspect of our nature. According to Malcolm Slavin (personal communication, 2010),

> This is not the id or instinctuality in Freud's sense, but rather a level of innate interconnectedness with the world that we partially lost (over several million years) when we 'traded' a far greater embeddedness in nature for our uniquely human capacity for language and the construction of meaning. This partial loss—this state of being in nature and apart from it[6]—endures

in us as an ongoing tension as well as a sense of something missing—a 'paradise lost'

As we came to rely increasingly on emotional, social, and mental skills, and less on innate physical and instinctual abilities, athletic and other bodily pursuits have become integral human activities. Our involvement in athletic play and other ritualized bodily activities—such as rock music and dance—may represent an ongoing, creative effort to retrieve our human connection with the larger natural world and "heal an unhealable breach at the core of our identity" (Slavin, personal communication, 2010).

As Freud (1930) recognized, the shift to creating complex social worlds and culture meant subordinating our passions and instincts—our wilder side—to reason. There is something wild, even risky, about sports. There are rules and boundaries, and raw physical aggression must be tempered by skill and strategy, but things can get out of control. People get hurt, sometimes killed, because of the danger inherent in the sport (football, skiing, boxing) or because of fans' or players' passions running amok (soccer stampedes, hockey and baseball brawls).

Far from being a light diversion from the real business of life or a sign of emotional immaturity, in many instances intense involvement in sports reveals and expresses an elemental and vital part of our nature. Sports, games, and intense bodily pursuits, as well as other activities, such as gardening, stargazing, and caring for and playing with pets, enable us to rediscover and retain our connection to an essential source of creativity and vitality, one with which we may always be vulnerable to losing touch.

Notes

1 Henceforth I will use "psychoanalyst" to refer to anyone who practices psychoanalytic therapy.
2 Sports and athletes—especially professionals—are also worshiped in our culture; my focus here is on one side of this dialectic.
3 Bill Littlefield (2010), host of the National Public Radio (NPR) sports show, "It's Only a Game," noted recently that "athletes are stereotyped for not being the sharpest tools in the box."
4 There is another compelling aspect of sports: unlike psychoanalytic work, excellence in sports is demonstrable and measurable; it can be consensually validated. In sports there are winners and losers, records that can be broken, and awards

based largely on objective data. Like music, it has a universal language that is understandable across space and time. Since most of life is more like psychoanalysis than sports—in the gray area—it is nice to have something unambiguous, or at least less ambiguous, in our lives. Few can argue with the claim that the NY Yankees are the greatest sports team in history; their 27 world championships are proof enough for most people.

5 My characterization of sports as physical is a matter of emphasis, since sports are more physically demanding than, say, psychoanalysis.

6 Deep engagement in sports may also provide a vantage point, perspective, and grounding that helps us stand apart from—or outside—our dominant culture or subculture. Psychoanalytic treatment itself can and often does provide something very similar. This may be valuable for many reasons; for one, it enables us to counter powerful pressures to conform unthinkingly and overly accommodate to prevailing norms. By capitalizing on what I view as a universal aspiration to stand apart from—and deeply engage with—culture, psychoanalysis may be able to recapture some of its former credibility, respect, and status (Greif, work in progress).

References

Brown, S.L. (1994), Animals at play. *National Geographic*, 186(6):2–35.

Freud, S. (1930), Civilization and its discontents. S*tandard Edition*, 21:64–145. London: Hogarth Press, 1961.

Greif, D. (2012), The revitalization of psychoanalysis: Antidote to 'instant culture. *Clinica e Investigacion Relacional: Revista electronica de Psicoterapia (Spanish journal)*, 6(1):56–63.

Hirsch, I. and Blumberg P. (2010), Introduction to special issue on intense involvement with sports. *Contemporary Psychoanalysis*, 46(4):475–479.

Kennedy Jr., E. (2009), Edward Kennedy Jr.'s and Patrick Kennedy's remembrance. August 29, www.nytimes.com/2009.

Lippmann, P. (2009), There ain't no cure for love. Presidential Address, William Alanson White Society Colloquium, September 25.

Littlefield, B. (2010), It's only a game. WBUR, National Public Radio, July 3, 2010.

Pinker, S. (2002), *The Blank Slate: The Modern Denial of Human Nature*. New York: Penguin Books.

Sandel, M.J. (2009), *Justice: What's the Right Thing to Do?* New York: Farrar, Straus & Giroux.

Winnicott, D.W. (1971), *Playing and Reality*. New York: Routledge.

Chapter 4

The sensibility of baseball
Structure, imagination, and the resolution of paradox

Stephen Seligman, D.M.H.

Sports evoke strong passions: awe and elation, depression and disgust, omnipotence and humiliation, grief and despair, urgent competitiveness, grandeur, even ecstasy and violence. All this needs no explanation for the devoted fan, but to the uninitiated and even the self-reflective *cognoscenti*, the devotion of the fans isn't matched by the games' real value.[1] "If asked where baseball stood amid such notions as country, family, love, art and religion, we might say derisively, 'Just a game'," wrote Thomas Boswell (1984) about his beloved sport. "But under oath, I'd abandon some of these before I'd give up baseball .... What is *baseball* doing here?" (p. 287).

Analysts are used to applying their particular expertise to such apparent incongruities to unmask the displacement of strong feeling and meaning. One typical approach invokes the concept of narcissistic identification with sports to build a theory of vicarious experience: The fan suspends the boundaries between himself and his heroes or team. Living through their successes and failures, he absorbs the grandeur he attributes to them and cushions feelings of inferiority and defeat by seeing them played out elsewhere. The fan can regress to the childhood world of good and bad, bigs and smalls, winners and losers, us and them: Instead, he seeks victory and triumph without the tragic inevitability of loss and defeat. Aggression and competition come out without the usual dangers, and he can feel part of something bigger, stronger and better than he really takes himself to be. A satisfying mix indeed.

There is much to be said for this type of analysis. But it also runs the risk of denying its objects' specific character and aesthetics. As with religion, art, and even politics, such interpretive strategies here may obscure the beauty, complexity, and creativity of some of the most ambitious human endeavors. At worst, they expropriate, rather than appreciate, what they examine in a triumphal evocation of the infantile that the nimble analyst can find almost anywhere. Examples of this are not hard to find: Jones's (1949) confounding of *Hamlet* and *Oedipus*; Bettelheim's (1968) reduction of 60s' college protesters to oedipal crybabies; and even Freud's (1910) inventive comments on Leonardo or religion all foreclose rather than illuminate the compelling forms and forces of their subjects.

Like Boswell, I am (ironically) skeptical that sports, even my beloved baseball, has the moral or aesthetic gravity of its counterparts. But I am also, I should confess, a committed sports fan, given to devotion to my favorite teams, awe at an elegant play, full-blown joy after a great game, and pronounced irritability, if not short-term depression, following even a trivial loss. I have little choice but to meet baseball on its own terms. Analysts, of course, do well to routinely meet our objects with such respect, even if we must call on our own expertise in the process. When we can allow ourselves to be so influenced, we have the best chance to be affected and even transformed by other fields that are at least as formidable as our own, rather than just impressing what we know on them. All this, of course, parallels the contemporary shift from the vision of the clinical analyst as one who knows to one who is dialogically creating new knowledge and, even more vitally, new experience.

The sensibility of baseball

Though some of it may apply more broadly, this chapter focuses on baseball's appeal, following my personal preference and immersion and also because, I hope to show, it is the most formally articulated and beautiful of the North American sports. There is a substantial and eloquent literature on this subject: The Library of America volume on baseball (Dawidoff, 2002), for example, includes contributions by Carl Sandburg, William Carlos Williams, Thomas Wolfe, Bernard Malamud, Robert Frost, John Updike, Philip Roth, Amiri Baraka, Richard Ford, Don DeLillo, and Stephen King, along with Stephen Jay Gould, Tallulah Bankhead, and a broad assortment of sportswriters, academics, and literate ballplayers. They share a recognition of an elegant integration of form and spaces, of special time and special times, of near-perfection amid the freedom of play, of dreaminess combined with the compelling sense that nothing else matters more. DeLillo (1991) wrote:

> Baseball, [she says] using the word to sum up a hundred happy abstractions, themes that flare to life in the crowd shout and diamond symmetry, in the details of a dusty slide. The word has resonance if you're American, a sense of shared heart and untranslatable lore ... to suggest the democratic clamor, a history of sweat and play on sun-dazed afternoons, an openness of form that makes the game a kind of welcome to my country.
>
> (pp. 8–9)

DeLillo conveys the depth and spaciousness of baseball, a sense of feeling, history and form not to be found elsewhere in sports (hardly imaginable in football, hockey, golf, or even basketball) and rarely elsewhere. Whitman (quoted in Dawidoff, 2002), a Brooklyn man before the Dodgers, is even more explicit: "[Baseball] has the snap, go, fling of the American atmosphere—belongs as much to our institutions, fits into them as significantly as our constitutions, laws: is just as important in the sum total of our historic life" (p. 1).

Unique among American sports, baseball evokes a refined devotion that seems to some like hyperbole, but that for others reaches toward its spirit to capture the enthusiasm and desire that it carries and contains: Its special gift is to contain paradox without resolving it. It offers an exceptional blend of harmony and stress, of time and timelessness, of spaciousness and confinement. Baseball calls forth purity and perfection without falling into the trap of claiming to attain them.[2] The baseball fan is offered the hope of redemption but even more frequently disillusioned. Highly plastic but carefully regulated, it maintains elegant balances of regularity and disorder, of predictability and suspense, of repetition and variety, and of seclusion from reality and compelling physical skill and substance.

Baseball, of course, has its own enclosed spaces—the infield, the field between the foul lines, and the ballpark itself, within which apparently divergent elements combine and interrelate to form larger wholes within which they nonetheless retain their sizes and shapes.

The eponymous central object of focal attention—the ball itself—is one of the smallest in all sports, while its container—the *ballpark*—is one of the largest. (Only golf, something of an individual skill game rather than a team sport, exceeds baseball in each regard.) Watching a baseball game requires a focus on small spaces (the base, the ball and the bat, the batter's box, the ball in the glove) amidst almost infinite domains (the outfield, much larger than the few fielders who spread out to "cover" it). The most dramatic gesture of all, the home run, exceeds the boundaries and clears the bases, leaving a clean, if newly contextualized, slate for the next pitcher-batter duo.[3] Moreover, the baseball field combines regularities and irregularities: Each infield's outline precisely corresponds to every other's (90 feet from each base to the next, but colorfully called a diamond, rather than a square), as does the distance from the spot from which the pitcher must pitch, the "rubber," to home plate (the oddly detailed, slightly irregular 60.6 inches), while every outfield has its own dimensions and shape. (One outfield even has a small, hilly rise.) The outfield configurations were briefly regularized (though never exactly standardized) during the decades from the 1960s through the 1980s, when utilitarian uniformity predominated in stadium construction, but happily this trend has been reversed in a series of distinctive parks with more old-fashioned character.

Thinking about all this, analysts might enliven our own ideas about "containment." We are used to thinking of the good analytic dyads as sites for the relatively benign exposure of psychological pain, chaos, and destruction; but they are also arenas to contain the paradoxes of form and order amidst freedom, chaos, constraint and frailty, the longing for creativity and illusion in the face of reality and the risks of phantasy (see Winnicott (1975) on this important distinction), and the like. We think of good analyses as disclosing, expanding, and integrating these, as they also provide protection from the nightmares and pressures that we are so used to thinking about (Winnicott, 1975; Carnochan, 2006).

Fields and rules

One way that psychoanalysis and baseball inform one another, then, is through their apparently paradoxical integration of freedom and structure. Analytic practice, even contemporary analysis, is highly regularized, if not ritualized. And, although it may have few rules, these may often seem arbitrary and even rigid: sessions always at the same time and with the same duration, often for years; the staunchly asymmetrical and often caricatured roles of analyst and analysand; unusually rigorous requirements for payment of fees, as when patients pay for all appointments, whether attended or not; the strictures against contact outside the office; and so on. Referring to these peculiar elements even as they understand how involved we are, several of my patients describe analysis as a "game," ironically conveying both contempt and awe.

Paradoxically, this regulated setup buttresses the general atmosphere of interpersonal safety, and potentiates the least restrictive and widest ranging discourse. Freud's (1914) prescription for the psychoanalytic relationship, albeit idealized, precludes action so that the imagination can have free reign: When things are so routinized and, in a sense, removed from the world of immediate material consequences, then emotions, memories, projections, and fantasies can emerge more richly than in ordinary life. Liminality enables inner freedom (Geertz, 1977; Hoffman, 1998). Since its foundation, psychoanalysis has been the original "field of dreams," at least for the 20th century.[4]

Baseball, on the other hand, has an exceptional array of elaborate and explicit rules. Detailed, comprehensive, covering every possible eventuality, these regulate a network of situations that organize and disperse, determined by a blend of athletic ability and chance. There are rules governing every situation (balls and strikes, bunts, running from bases and stealing them, when to leave the base after a fly ball has been caught, and so on), and, in fact, these rules create those situations. Taken together, these rules create an intricate set of dimensions and forms within which the players' actions take on their meaning.

Situations and decisions

Organized by the rules and the ballfield's spaces, then, players' performances generate an unfolding series of situations. Some are repetitive and even desultory, but others coalesce into high drama and significance. Moment-to-moment uncertainty and suspense flux through regularity, often defined by an endless series of apparently minor variations and details.

For example, the batter reaches base on a fourth ball by refraining from swinging at a pitch just a few millimeters off the strike zone; gets to second base on a sacrifice bunt (an intentionally soft, slow effort to bat a ball just in front of home plate) when the pitcher decides at the last microsecond to toss the ball to first base instead of taking the risk of getting that lead runner at second. Now a baserunner, he steals third by sliding in under the tag, which was just an inch too high as the second baseman has to reach up for the catcher's quick but just slightly errant throw, and is then thrown out at home plate when the outfielder's one-bounce throw following a shallow fly ball reaches the catcher just where he has planted his burly and padded body, one step up the baseline blocking the runner's path. (There is a rule, by the way, governing when runners can leave bases after fly balls, how fielders can block runners' access to bases, and when runners can run the fielders over without being called out for "interference.")

Such situations are both familiar and novel to experienced fans. They have seen most of these plays before, but never with quite the same players or in quite the same patterns: the one-bounce throw with the only somewhat speedy runner, the burly or not so burly catcher, and so on. Players and fans alike exercise their technical expertise around these moments, both in anticipation and in retrospect: Should the runner go on the fly ball? How fast is he? How strong is the center fielder's throwing arm? Or, afterward, should he have gone? As in psychoanalysis (and many other fields, for that matter), whether or not the decision was a good one is finally a matter not of outcome, but of how proper factors were considered. Not everything can be anticipated. Style comes in here, too: Some teams will live and die by speed; others will wait for the big hit. There are various methods, including some very articulated statistics, to approach these questions (few Major League dugouts are without computers these days), but they remain as much a matter of experience, hunch, and even aesthetics as of quantitative analysis.

In-game judgment depends on a subtle understanding of these situations. It is, for example, a canonical view that in a close game the runner should not take a chance at being thrown out while trying to score from third on a sacrifice fly with *no outs* when there is a relatively high probability that one of the next batters will provide a more certain scoring opportunity; but the runner should go with *one out* when that probability is reduced and so the opportunity cost is effectively lowered. (If there are two outs, the inning is over once the ball has been caught.) Even this may vary, however, depending on further situational factors, which contextualize the ones already in place (here, the number of outs in the inning): the score and how late in the game; who's running, pitching, hitting next, and the like.

In the final inning of the fourth game of the 2003 National League Championship Series, with the Giants one out from elimination, their sharp-hitting, but slow-moving first baseman J.T. Snow was on second base, in position to score a game-prolonging run on an base hit to the outfield. But, on the next at bat, he was thrown out at the plate on a bouncing single to shallow left field, ending the game and the Giants' chances to play in the World Series that year. A faster runner might well have beaten the throw. Felipe Alou, the Giants' manager, explained that he would have substituted a pinch-runner for Snow if his had been the winning run, but not the tying run, since he would need Snow's strong hitting if the game were to continue. Right or wrong, Alou's call was reasonable and respected, albeit heartbreaking for the Giants.

Moe Berg (1941), a solid Major League catcher with degrees from Princeton and Columbia Law, echoed this sentiment in describing catchers' and pitchers' collaborative decision-making about which pitch to throw to which hitter:

> The catcher has to make quick decisions, bearing in mind the score, the inning, the number of men on the bases, and other factors. ... The pitcher tries not to ... give the hitter the ball he hits best. But it is also dangerous to over-refine. Taking the physical as well as the psychological factors into consideration, the pitcher must at times give even the best hitter his best pitch under the circumstances. He pitches hard, lets the law of averages do its work, and never second-guesses himself.
>
> (pp. 176–177)

These things can become even more nuanced. Weather conditions, for example, can affect the situation: I once watched a Red Sox game at Boston's Fenway Park, where the threat of an impending game-ending downpour in the seventh inning pushed the visiting Indians, who were trailing by a run, to send a not-so-fast runner from second to third to get into a better position to score. Although he might well have been thrown out, the risk had to be taken since this now appeared likely to be the last chance to get the tying run home.[5]

Baseball and its situations, then, are composed of fairly complex interactions between multiple variables and structures. Shaped by the rules, the field, the players' skills, and so on, specific dimensions (like the number of outs, the inning, the rain, and so on) will affect the meaning of every particular. Berg (1941) again:

> The pitcher may throw overhand to take full advantage of the white shirts in the bleacher background. Breaking balls are more effective when thrown against the resistance of the wind. In the latter part of the day, when shadows are cast in a stadium ball park, the pitcher may change his tactics by throwing more fast balls than he did earlier in the game.
> (p. 177)

In both passages, Berg captures the uncertain tenor of decision making in nonlinear dynamic systems, where the relationships between multiple factors shift as the factors themselves change, all, in turn, affecting those particular factors as well as the subsequent development of the situation. Such processes are usually so complex as to make prediction very difficult, if not impossible, since there are too many interrelated moving parts to track all at once and the patterns by which they interrelate can change at any moment. Weather conditions, for example, can be steady for days, if not weeks, but at certain moments, as, for example, when the clouds are saturated with a critical amount of moisture, the system shifts to rain, then stops, and starts again, and so on, with the next set of events very hard to predict as the rain itself cools the clouds, they screen the sun intermittently, and so on. (See Seligman, 2005, among others, for a discussion of nonlinear dynamic systems theories and their relevance for psychoanalysis.)

Similarly, each baseball game and, indeed, each season, consists of unfolding patterns of emerging situations, often punctuating extended intervals where nothing game-changing happens. Psychoanalysts are familiar with the flux of dynamic shifts amid such doldrums, often lasting days, weeks, or even months. For some, these rhythms feed boredom, but for others, and on the best days, such punctuated flow is at the heart of something deep and engrossing. Becoming engrossed in the apparently mundane, knowing that, under the right conditions, it may unexpectedly give rise to something of great significance, offers special rewards.[6]

Baseball time

Competitive sports have their own narrative forms, and, as I have said, competitive games may offer their own master narrative, actualizing the idealized version of bipolar conflict in which there is a winner and a loser (war, elections, the unmourned Oedipus Complex, for example). With regard to temporality, each sport has its particular way of organizing, and thus implicitly narrating, time, ways in which each game begins, evolves, and ends: Each has its own way of playing with temporal plasticity. The last two minutes of a close football or basketball game feel very different from the first two, for example, and the "extra time" of a soccer match can feel like an eternity for a team protecting a one-goal lead.

Many sports define their games' temporal span by ordinary clock time—*chronos*, in which time moves forward in more or less fixed and ordinary units, like seconds, minutes, and so on: The "periods" of the other major sports—American football, soccer, basketball, hockey are all defined by length in minutes, and it is within these parameters that they play with time. Others subordinate time to the point tally; volleyball and tennis, for example, have no "clock," just scores that, when reached, mark the end of a game, set, match, and so on, triggering the recurrence of the last temporal unit of a sequence (game, set) or the end of a match altogether. In some others, the clock itself is the measure—track and field, swimming, speed skating. In whichever case, the variables that move the game along refer to something that is fixed outside the game itself—numbers, units of objective time, and the like.

But baseball is, as far as I know, the only sport that proposes its own temporal units independent of both the score and running time—the pitch, the at-bat, the half inning, the inning, even the batting order. Baseball is the game without a clock. Ordinary time is suspended into a series of moments, punctuated by the physical facts of pitching, batting, catching, throwing, and running, coming together in the field organized by its few physical boundaries and the rules that give form and meaning to the players' movements. Similarly, the physical movements that constitute the game are varied, multidirectional, and relatively spontaneous. Whereas in most sports there is a forward direction in which the ball is carried, thrown, or struck, there is no single direction in baseball. The pitcher throws the ball in one direction, the batter tries to "turn it around," and then the fielders move in all directions to chase down the ball and throw it in just as many, and so on. Moreover, strength, distance, and even precision are not enough; the motions of the game are fraught with chance and even a random quality, and as such, with the hint of tragedy: The long fly ball that *almost* clears the stands; the ground ball that gets just under the fielder's glove; the line drive hit as hard as a ball can be hit, but right at a fielder.[7]

Baseball thus has an unusually creative relationship with time, as well as with space. Its deliberate pace, while tedious for some, allows for reflection and interest that are usually precluded in the other sports. Baseball is nothing if not a game of expectation, anticipation, and even prediction. Moment to moment and over the longer spans of the game and the season, the pitcher and the catcher have to know which pitches the batter hits well in general, along with the last pitch that batter hit; the batter needs to remember which pitch the pitcher has been relying on in which situations; the fielder keeps in mind how speedy each runner is; the manager tracks how the current pitcher does against the next batter; and so on. The experienced fan empathizes with these decisions on the field, frequently imagines making them himself, and often knows the statistics most relevant to the business at hand.

The elegance and accuracy of baseball statistics and the inner forms of the game

The special character of baseball statistics reflects the transparency, precision, and organization of the game while preserving its dynamic complexity and unfolding spontaneity. Even as it is the most lyrical of the major North American sports, baseball is also the most accessible and precisely available to quantitative measurement. Its statistics are the most eloquent and detailed in sports, by leaps and bounds, in tracking players' abilities and, in general, situations, effects, and outcomes. An innovative generation of quantitative analysts has developed complex, computer-aided metrics that take the already refined systems to a new level. For example, one statistic proposes to measure the comparative effect of different fielders' ability to play their positions; the model compares the number of offensive runs scored or hits to the area of the player's position while the player is in the game to the average while the same pitchers were pitching. If there were, say, 0.5 runs fewer scored and 1.3 hits fewer to left field (I'm making this one up) per game while slugger Barry Bonds played there than when other Giants were playing, his value to the team would be increased by that much even if his formidable hitting lagged in any particular season during which he was receiving his multimillion dollar salary. Even such long-established measures as earned-run average (number of runs allowed by a pitcher per nine innings pitched, discounting those due to fielding errors) and slugging percentage (total bases obtained on batted balls and walks, corrected for bases obtained on errors, divided by number of times at bat) have face validity and precision that eclipses those of other sports, such as the relatively weak passing ratings in football or even points per game in basketball.[8]

Despite their range, however, the baseball statistics still leave one or another imponderable unaccounted for. Baseball's statistics have only general predictive value. Rather than following the hyper-quantifying empiricist's drive to reduce the dynamic vitality of human situations to standardizable parts, baseball's statistics don't drain its integrity, but instead are another index of how the game blends complexity, regularity and unpredictability.

Memory in the field

Moreover, even as devoted fans are well aware of the players' records, they remain absorbed in the unfolding spectacle on the field. No matter how precisely the game's patterns can be recorded quantitatively, baseball fans are also immersed in memory of different sorts. The games evoke the lived experience of the past as they create a new present, bringing to mind the familiar forms in new variations in which the old ones are altered and re-arrayed. Most fans know some of the sport's history, its situations, teams, players. Since most have played the game, there is the immediate physical identification, the internal mirroring of every gesture—the swinging bat hitting the ball, the step out of the batter's box, the ball in the glove, the throw to the base, and on and on. Other sports may evoke the same memorial and historical feelings, but they usually move too fast and their situations are not so well defined as to allow quite so much memory to flow in, explicitly and implicitly, for time to stop and rearrange, to open up and re-saturate.

Recent neurocognitive research about "mirror neurons" has shown that the motor neurons involved in making specific movements, whether taking an ordinary step or swinging a bat, are activated when a person *observes someone else making those movements but is not making them herself.* They call the observer's emerging inner experience of something quite like what he or she would feel when making the movement (even as it is not actually enacted), "embodied simulation" (Gallese, 2009).

Following this model, we can imagine a baseball spectator actually feeling the player's motion at bat, throwing the ball, and so on. This kinesthetic identification is spontaneous, instantaneous, and, inasmuch as so many fans have played the game, often roughly accurate and also very evocative: The fan feels that he is in the game even though he knows that he is watching it, all the while recalling his own days as a player. Passion and nostalgia are aroused as they are both overcome and sustained in the special circumstance of the bounded ball field and the paradox of identification and distance in the spectator role.

All this becomes focused and vitalized in the gripping moment when the situation organizes into heightened significance—the close game, men on base, tying run in scoring position. Even in a slow game, there is the chance for the expanse in which not much is happening to coalesce into high drama. In the more heightened moments in which a game, or even a season, hangs in the balance, the most compelling and momentous emotions emerge in epic proportion. Bartlett Giamatti (1977), then a Yale literature Professor, later to be President of that university and eventually Commissioner of Baseball, wrote about a climactic moment, in which his beloved Red Sox's season could either be prolonged by a hit or ended by an out from their batter, Jim Rice:

> Rice the best clutch hitter on the club ... so quick and strong he once checked his swing halfway through and snapped the bat in two ... the sound was overwhelming, fathers pounded their sons on the back, cars pulled off the road, households froze, New England exulted in its blessedness ... for Rice and a summer stretching halfway through October. Briles [the pitcher] threw, Rice swung, and it was over. One pitch, a fly to center, and it stopped. Summer died in New England, and like rain slipping off a roof, the crowd slipped out of Fenway, quickly. ... Mutablility had turned the seasons and translated hope to memory once again.
>
> (p. 12)[9]

Such compelling moments call forth the game's magic in the suspension of the ordinary forward temporal flux, leaving a kind of free-floating attention into which the mundane dimensions mingle with the broad contours of the life course, of history and grief, of everlasting youth and hope, evanescence, and fragility.

Baseball gets better with time. Compared with some of the even more spontaneous sports (like basketball) or the more regulated (like football), it is not so reliant on either streamlined situations or regression to more simple or heroic forms. Instead, it brings forth the longing for an integrative resonance of present and past in a medium in which time flows not by the clock, but along lines defined by the actions of the players as they are situated in the playing field and the rules. Hopeful and tragic, nostalgic and spontaneous, its time is fluid and plastic but nonetheless flows forward inexorably: The inning *will* end when the third out is recorded and the game *will* end when the team with fewer runs has used all its chances. But the hope that time can stop and it can all last forever remains on the edge of the game's magical moments, which are not so uncommon there as in most other precincts.[10] Giamatti (1977) captured this poignantly after he described Rice's season-ending fly ball:

[Baseball] breaks my heart because it was meant to, because it was meant to foster in me again the illusion that there was something abiding, some pattern and some impulse that could come together to make a reality that would resist the corrosion; and because, after it had fostered again that most hungered-for-illusion, the game was meant to stop, and betray precisely what it promised. ... there are those who were born with the wisdom to know that nothing lasts. These are the truly tough among us, the ones who can live without illusion, or even the hope of illusion. I am not that grown-up or up-to-date. I need to think something lasts forever, and it might as well be that state of being that is a game; it might as well be that, in a green field, in the sun.

(pp. 12–13)

Afterthought: baseball and clinical psychoanalysis: common dimensions in contrasting format

Baseball and psychoanalytic practice mirror one another in both symmetrical and inverted ways. They share some common dimensions—the prominence of rules in shaping open, safe, illusory environments; detachment from actuality to sustain hyper-reality; creating their own internal and highly plastic senses of time; sustaining extended periods of quiescence punctuated by moments of heightened significance and drama.

Each reflects the variability and fluidity of the fluxes and spaces of everyday life, at the same time that they restrict the scope and potential for disorder: They are unpredictable, messy, often chaotic, but not that much. Both baseball and psychoanalysis are complex and unpredictable enough to feel "real" but constrained enough to contain the most acute senses of threat and danger so as to allow for imagination and emotional freedom.

The few rules of analysis support the formation of a highly protected environment where some of the most important personal themes can come to life, creating a seclusion within which moments that may be trivial to the outsider feel crucial to those inside. Similarly, though in a different key, as the game plays out in its bounded space, the multiple rules of baseball combine with its open variability to construct a special emotional and sensory area in which little else matters and everything seems to be at stake, in a materialized reverie made to be shared with others (the "field of dreams"). There are enough rules to simulate, or at least imitate, a bit of the complexity of actual life, but far fewer uncertainties and organizing patterns, which allows for a sense of comfort and repose. All this is sustained in a set of patterned and interrelated dynamisms of movements and spaces, changing over time but relatively stable and contained.

Good psychoanalyses and good baseball games sustain a supple, fluid balance among uncertainty and predictability, structure and indefiniteness, freedom and constraint. Baseball has many rules and clinical psychoanalysis just a few, but each is the most variegated, vital, and lifelike form in its domain, baseball among spectator sports and analysis among the psychotherapies. Each establishes a framework for evoking and deepening the sense of heightened consequence and authenticity. Analysis and baseball, like other forms of illusion, such as art and religion, evoke the prospect of a hyper-reality which can be transformative—baseball's in the shorter run, analysis' in the longer. Both tantalize with the hint of eternal renewal and the suspension of loss and nostalgia: In both baseball and analysis, there is always another day. But therein lies the difference, for the sport is, after all, a game on a (usually) outdoor field of play, set up for pleasure rather than something more pragmatic and consequential. But there is not about to be another life, and for most, not another analysis.

Notes

1 Sports, of course, is a multibillion dollar international business, whose corporate beneficiaries are well aware of this coin of their realm. *Contemporary Psychoanalysis*, Vol. 46, No. 4. ISSN 0010–7530 © 2010 William Alanson White Institute, New York, NY. All rights reserved.
2 In official baseball terminology, the word "perfect" is applied to one specific situation, a game in which a pitcher allows no runners to reach base—27 batters, 27 outs. While over 250,000 games have been played in Major League Baseball since its inception in 1903, fewer than 25 perfect games have been pitched. And no one believes that these games are actually "perfect," since not all pitches are strikes and not all the batters strike out.

3 Except when it ends the game, in what may be the most dramatic of all baseball moments—the "walk-off" home run. DeLillo's (1997) incomparable account of Bobby Thomson's *season-ending* home run in 1951 is one of the most remarkable examples of all baseball writing.

4 Is baseball—organized in its current Major League form in 1903, three years after Freud's (1900) *magnum opus, Interpretation of Dreams,* was published—psychoanalysis' democratic American counterpart? Both fell from hegemony with the advent of the corporate hypercapitalism of the 1970s: baseball, to the mechanical brutalism of football; analysis, to the objectifying, fast-acting efficiencies of psychopharmacology and other imaginative psychotherapies.

5 When Boswell (1984) writes, "When we meet a bona fide fan—and baseball fanciers can be as snobbish as wine sippers or prize rose gardeners—we start from an assumption of kinship" (p. 288) he is referring to the fraternity of those who grasp the nuances of such technical and historical appraisals. Shortly after the rain-soaked Fenway game, I asked a nine-year-old relatively new to the game about the Indians' decision. His impeccable and extensive response showed that he understood the depth and intricacy of the matter, an analytic aptitude for following the moving parts in a complex situation borne out in his talent, years later, for urban planning (Daniel Kazin, personal communication).

6 Stephen Jay Gould and his colleagues' (Eldredge & Gould, 1972; Gould, 1989) term "punctuated equilibrium" applies well to such processes. Gould, a very serious baseball fan as well as one of the foremost contemporary evolutionary theorists, proposed that evolution has proceeded by relatively long periods of stability, in which few new species or decisively altered adaptive characteristics arise, are interrupted by moments in which key genetic changes have been organized into new life forms. In proposing this model, Gould overturned the commonplace view of evolution as a linear process, with new mutations integrated into some existing organisms while others wane owing to their competitive disadvantage. Instead, entire genetic lines die out rather suddenly, in game-changing moments in which the ecological systems seem to shift dramatically. Gould was among the many contemporary scientists who relied on nonlinear dynamic systems theories to capture the uneven and chaotic, but systematic, flux and flow of natural and social systems.

7 The final out of the seventh and final game of 1962 World Series came when Yankees' second baseman Bobby Richardson raised his glove as if to protect himself reflexively and caught Giants slugger Willie McCovey's streaking line drive. If the ball had been hit inches to the right or left, it would most likely have gone through to the outfield and tied the game, prolonging the Giants' chance to score the winning run or at

least, sending the game into extra innings. As it stood, the Yankees won the World Championship in that instant.

After the game, McCovey was asked about his reaction. "A man hits the ball as hard as he can," he said. "He can't feel bad about what he does. Of course you want to win. Of course you'd rather hit one off the fists and break your bat and have it drop in, but if you hit it hard, that's all you can do"(quoted in Hirsch, 2010, p. 374).

8 I once went to a ballgame with a Swiss quantitative research psychologist who was seeing baseball for the first time. She couldn't follow the game, but when she grasped the statistical framework, she was fascinated and found her way into the action on the field from the point of view of probabilities and the like.
9 One of Giamatti's best-known books is *The Earthly Paradise and the Renaissance Epic* (1966).
10 Some analyses go on too long, even indefinitely, when the analyst and analysand avoid realizing that there are often benefits to treating the illusory as time limited.

References

Berg, M. (1941), Pitchers and catchers. In: *Baseball: A Literary Anthology*, ed. N. Dawidoff. New York: Library of America, 2002, pp. 165–177.

Bettelheim, B. (1968), (quoted in) The generation gap. *LIFE*, May17.

Boswell, T. (1984), *Why Time Begins on Opening Day*. New York: Penguin Books.

Carnochan, P. (2006), Containers without lids. *Psychoanalytic Dialogues*, 6:341–362.

Dawidoff, N. ed. (2002), *Baseball: A Literary Anthology*. New York: Library of America.

DeLillo, D. (1991), *Mao II*. New York: Penguin Books.

DeLillo, D. (1997), *Underworld*. New York: Simon & Schuster.

Eldredge, N. & Gould, S.J. (1972), Punctuated equilibria: An alternative to phyletic gradualism. In: *Models in Paleobiology*, ed. T.J.M. Schopf. San Francisco, CA: Freeman Cooper, pp. 82–115.

Freud, S. (1900), *Interpretation of Dreams. Standard Edition*, 4 & 5. London: Hogarth Press, 1953.

Freud, S. (1910), Leonardo da Vinci and a memory of his childhood. *Standard Edition*, 11:63–138. London: Hogarth Press, 1957.

Freud, S. (1914), Remembering, repeating and working through. *Standard Edition*, 12:145–156. London: Hogarth Press, 1958.

Gallese, V. (2009), Mirror neurons, embodied simulation, and the neural basis of social identification. *Psychoanalytic Dialogues*, 19:519–536.

Geertz, C. (1977), *Interpretation of Cultures: Selected Essays.* New York: Basic Books.
Giamatti, A.B. (1966), *The Earthly Paradise and the Renaissance Epic.* New York: Norton, 1989.
Giamatti, A.B. (1977), The green fields of the mind. In: *A Great and Glorious Game: Baseball Writings of A. Bartlett Giamatti,* ed. K.S. Robson. Chapel Hill, NC: Algonquin Books of Chapel Hill, pp. 7–14, 1998.
Gould, S.J. (1989), *Wonderful Life: The Burgess Shale and the Nature of History.* New York: Norton.
Hirsch, J.S. (2010), *Willie Mays: The Life, The Legend.* New York: Scribner.
Hoffman, I.Z. (1998), *Ritual and Spontaneity in the Psychoanalytic Process: A DialecticalConstructivist View.* Hillsdale, NJ: Analytic Press.
Jones, E. (1949), *Hamlet and Oedipus: A Classic Study in the Psychoanalysis of Literature.* New York: Doubleday Anchor.
Seligman, S. (2005), Dynamic systems theories as a metaframework for psychoanalysis. *Psychoanalytic Dialogues,* 15:285–319.
Winnicott, D.W. (1975), *Through Paediatrics to Psycho-Analysis: Collected Papers.* New York: Brunner/Mazel, 1992.

Chapter 5

Serve, smash, and self-states[1]
Tennis on the couch and courting
Steve Mitchell

Jean Petrucelli, Ph.D.

One only need contemplate the histrionics of tennis greats such as Ilie Nastase, Jimmy Connors, and John McEnroe to understand that, for most, tennis is a game in name only. In the vernacular, these players, like so many weekend players who regularly haunt any tennis center, would fall under the rubric "head cases." The world of tennis can be split into two camps—in one, players like Chris Evert and Pete Sampras calmly surmount the vicissitudes of trying to master that yellow spheroid object; in the other, players like Jimmy Connors, John McEnroe, and Serena Williams wear their emotions on their tennis sleeves. And then there are those who start in one camp and cross over to the other.

For example, few people know that Roger Federer was once considered an "ill tempered rogue," difficult though it may be to reconcile this image with his current persona. Crying when things went poorly; Federer would send his racket skidding across the court after an error. On occasion he would whine at bad calls, slam balls in anger, and argue with his father. The composed on-court demeanor that has come to define Federer as the personification of gracious sportsmanship stands in stark contrast to his early years as a young professional player. Even the legendary Bjorn Borg began as an "enfant terrible," a hot-headed player who, as he matured, became known as the "ice man" for his implacable behavior. Both supremely talented players learned to "control their emotions," gain sturdier mental approaches, and convert their pure skill into greatness.

Some players achieve this emotional transformation; some do not. In the 2009 US Open we witnessed the remarkable return of

Kim Clijsters, who became the first unseeded player to win the women's title. Her triumph was overshadowed by the inappropriate behavior of defending champion Serena Williams, who lost her cool and, in the process, her title to Clijsters. The pressure, mind games, mental strength, aggressiveness—passivity that athletes experience are usually the factors that tip the scale in the match, surmounting even the technical and tactical abilities of these players. We have probably all seen intelligent, successful people cursing and throwing their racquets on the tennis court; even if they control themselves we can easily spot their emotional dysregulation. It is rare, though, to see the ferocity of verbal abuse toward linesman or umpire delivered by a female athlete. In a tirade, Serena Williams stepped far outside the realm of acceptable behavior for female athletes with the intensity and dysregulation of her anger on the court at the US Open 2009. In doing so, she joined the historically reserved "men's only club" whose members are the likes of Ilie Nastase, Jimmy Conners, and John McEnroe—players who became legendary for their rampages against line judges, umpires, and each other. The common challenge that all these great players faced was controlling their tempers while harnessing their amazing competitive fires.

What is it that allows some players to regulate their emotions while performing such physically demanding feats? How can these players trust their subjective experience without becoming affectively dysregulated, and losing sustained concentration? What role does the body have in making those decisions for us? The body is not just a blank slate. It encodes and draws on its own procedural memories and encodes them in a way that sometimes gives the body "a mind of its own."

Let me also confess at the outset that on the tennis court I, too, am a "head case." Not the racquet-throwing, yelling-at-the-linesman- Serena kind, but the internally emotionally dysregulated kind, where I quietly do a beat-up job on myself, giving my opponent many "gifts" (points) in the process. The challenge, as I see it, is to deconstruct psychologically the process that creates the head case, which might repair my own tennis game at the same time (a rather daunting task, I must admit). How can the game of tennis transform a seemingly well-balanced person into a seething, name-calling (internal or external), self-doubting, head-down, racquet-tossing (not I, for the record) hellion? And what, if anything, can psychoanalysis and our understanding of affect regulation, dissociation, and the body and its performance contribute to answering this question? How does an athlete access the optimum self-state to excel in competition where "just enough" anxiety enhances performance?

Mind–body ... body–mind

As a psychoanalyst and avid tennis player myself, I realize how thinking affects our bodies' abilities and, conversely, how our bodily based memories affect our thinking so that both bodily and cognitively based experience mutually influence tennis performance. Playing tennis is a mind–body experience, but it is also the reverse—a body–mind experience in which the body tells us what the mind does not yet know. Sometimes these body–mind and mind–body processes work in sync and sometimes they cannot.

My tennis experiences have run the gamut from my being held hostage to the intruder in my head to playing "out of my mind." I started playing tennis late by today's standards, at age 13. But I took to the game quickly, was a ball girl at many US Open tournaments (Forest Hills and Flushing Meadows center stadium), played an exhibition set with Billie Jean King and Virginia Wade the first year of the NY Apples, went to college on a tennis scholarship, and have continued to play recreationally and competitively by USTA standards. Throughout, I have understood that one's psychological conflicts are often played out in the arena of tennis—be they conflicts relating to aggressiveness, competitiveness, anger, desire, fear, courage, risk taking, insecurity, distractibility, focus, fight or flight. Undoubtedly though, there is always, that moment on the court when "something happens" and, within a fraction of a second, my tournament training and strategies collide with emotions that overwhelm my mind. My promise to stay centered disintegrates. I get stuck in a moment and I can't get out of it.

I am told I am not alone in this conundrum. A reporter for the 2009 US Tennis Open, commenting on Dinara Safina's multiple double faults, said, "Her mind is in the way. She's just terrified" (Crouse, 2009, p. A1). Another reporter responding to this match stated, "It's like I cringe when people are serving second serves on key points. You can see it in their faces—it's almost like their mind is freezing up and they just look like they're not going to win the point" (p. A1).

I have often wondered if the "mind freezing up" is the hallmark of a dissociative moment for an athlete. It is a discordant moment when the link between how one thinks one can perform (the potential for performance) and how one physically experiences and creates this performance are not in sync. Players who may ultimately stand a far better chance of mentally staying in the game are those that can actively engage with their knowledge of capability (e.g., "I've successfully hit this shot in the past") and with their actual physical playing in a given moment while maintaining a sense of self-coherence. To be able simultaneously to hold the fear of losing while maintaining the motivating drive and desire to win requires tolerating both self-states, creating a convergence of different sensibilities. That ability may account for players of lesser skills sometimes beating more skilled ones simply by playing "smarter" (for example, 17-year-old Melanie Oudin beating Maria Sharapova in US Open 2009 Round Four and again, in Round Five, defeating Nadia Petrova). I also wonder if, for some players, dissociation can be adaptive, that is, used as a successful defense against the trauma of remembering lost matches or a series of missed points. When a player feels that parts of his or her game are falling apart, that may be the moment when the body, with its own encoded memories, overrides the mind and makes decisions for the player: every point is a new game and clearing the mind enhances athletic performance. It's the clutch experience rather than the choke—adaptive dissociation well honed.

Clutching or choking

Clutching or choking—life's dynamics can be experienced on the tennis court. How one responds on the court mirrors many reactions to outside life experiences, whether one is dealing with the subjective perception of line calls (when it can seem that one's reality or experience of "truth" is in question) or with the thousand split-second decisions that need to be made automatically in a match. The weighing of one's sense of self-worth or identity can hang in the balance each step of the way.

For most athletes there are internal and external events that can disturb one's concentration, one's self-regulating state of homeostasis, one's body performance, and one's effort. I am curious about the athlete's inner experience—the struggles around identity and self-worth based on performance; the conflicts over competition; the fear of success; the inner critical voices that disrupt affect regulation, thereby diminishing athletic performance. Did I just dump an easy forehand into the net because I'm still focused on the previous backhand that I missed? Or am I in more global distress, losing confidence in my competence as a human being? Or is my brain just not capable of self-reflection in a moment because of my heightened affective neurobiological state where I'm overwhelmed and not able to calmly reflect? There are times when I feel my body informs me of things my logical mind has yet to know, yet there are also times when my felt sense of physical unreliability and discontinuity fails to provide an ongoing experience of a body that can perform adequately during the rigors of the match. Is this the place where tennis and psychoanalysis meet at the net?

What is requisite for you to perform at the top of your game? On the tennis court, mental toughness and fierce competitiveness require you to remember that your strongest defense is to attack, so that your opponent becomes consciously involved in meeting your attack and thus has less time to formulate his or her own system. The first rule of thumb is to take chances when you are behind, never when ahead, because risks are worth taking only when you have everything to win and nothing to lose. The second rule of thumb is never to let your opponent know you are worried, fatigued, or in pain, for such knowledge will only give him or her confidence. I remember my tennis coach telling me to smile (I have a tendency to look serious while concentrating) even when feeling bad because a smile conveys an impression of confidence that shakes your opponent.

Do you see what I see?

Yet it is physiological arousal that truly hampers an athlete's performance—too much or too little is deleterious. Every athlete varies in how much arousal is ideal for peak performance. Tennis, unlike continuous action sports, is a combination of balancing the regulation of playing time and of "dead" time. Playing time is very demanding on a person's mental abilities since the action is fast paced and requires split-second reflexes and decisions as well as preparation and anticipation for the next shot. During "dead" time (which can be 60%–90% of the time the player is on the court) a player is not hitting the ball. In addition, the visual system finds it difficult to deal with abrupt changes, and changes in time also affect bodily rhythm, which influences tennis performance. Negotiating such moments successfully enable a player to be in the "ideal state" by regulating states of arousal There are, nevertheless, many thoughts and perceptions that may influence a move from the "ideal" state to the far less adaptive overactivated or under-activated body–mind state, which can adversely affect play.

We could argue from a neurobiological perspective that hyperarousal produces a lack of clarity and that decisions that then arise in our consciousness are consequently based on an "emotional mind" rather than logical thought. This emotional mind is expressed through bodily based actions that usurp the place of more complexly organized body–mind integrations. The emotional mind finds its home in the body, where the body then acts as if it has a mind of its own. Is the body–mind taking over then? For example, instead of playing a solid cross-court shot in defense, one might go for the corner down the line (a lower percentage shot where the tactical mind has been overridden); or, instead of just artfully putting a ball away on a sitter (a short ball that floats without pace), one might hit with full power at the line to prove something to the opponent. This response undoubtedly leads one to make many unforced errors—mistakes where the tactically wrong solution is chosen because we perform our strokes solely at the mercy of the body's arousal and its influence on our tactical responsiveness. To some players, the infinite possibilities in tennis create a sense of calm and inner peace. To other players, the complexity of choices—type of shot or placement on the court—becomes affectively overwhelming.

This state occurs, for example, in doubles play when a player cannot break out of his or her own perceptual mindset to achieve a sense of intersubjectivity with his or her partner. Internally overwhelmed, the player may disagree with the partner. In such a moment, the experience of what the player feels to be true as a subjective phenomenon often collides with what may be accurate on the court. The mediation of the forces involved in tennis—affect regulation and interpersonal relatedness—is also complicated by matters of perceptual accuracy, time, and space. The interplay of these factors on the court is individually felt, but also mutually experienced between members of a doubles team and often is visible to their opponents. This interplay of factors not only affects the outcome of play but also becomes manifest in those whom we affectionately refer to as "head cases."

Tennis legend John McEnroe's famous outburst, "You cannot be serious!" in Wimbledon, circa 1981, occurred when a shot was ruled out. This incident took place long before the Hawkeye's electronic monitor, which can now present a reliable, measurable, accurate truth. But most of us play without the benefit of this advanced technology, and our human visual processing decisions are emotionally laden with interpersonal consequences. There are times when life and death seem to hang in the balance of a line call, and the perception of a call questions the meaning of truth. Perceptual distortions can affect one's very sense of "going on being" (Winnicott, 1958) and create the need to switch self-states or dissociate the unbearable feeling of not being believed. To some, the moment can be experienced as a kind of referendum on their self-worth (Bromberg, 2009), especially in doubles play, in which "in syncness" is crucial. Your partner has a different perceptual experience and disagrees with you—your partner sees the ball out while you have seen it in.

Research now shows that tennis players and refs are much more likely to make a mistake by calling a good shot out than by calling a bad shot in (Whitney et al., 2008). This discrepancy occurs because, when objects travel faster than the human eye and brain can precisely track—for example, a 150-mile-an-hour serve (not mine)—one must fill in the gap in one's perception. In doing so, one tends to overshoot the object's actual location and think it traveled slightly farther than it did. These studies have added to the growing knowledge of how the human eye and brain misperceive objects moving at a high speed. To a tennis player, these studies strongly suggest which calls are worth challenging and which are best left alone.

Human visual processing has interpersonal ramifications as well and requires strategies to determine which calls in the game we choose to challenge. In our psychological work, we do not base our thinking on absolutes. In tennis there are absolutes on which individuals do not necessarily agree. The ball is either in or out. However, the subjective experience of a ball being "seen" as in or out can change the outcome of the match, ruin a friendship, or generate feelings of doubt and mistrust in any player. A ball that is seen as "in" by the player but "out" by the umpire (or opponent or doubles partner) can represent a violation of one's sense of justice, because the umpire (or "other") should have seen the ball as "in" according to the rules. The science of perception brings a new factor into play, and recent studies show us clearly that the body plays a huge role in what we tend to think of as mental experience.

Visualization

Tennis performance, however, is not just about increased affect tolerance—although it could be argued that to play "in the zone" requires a negotiation of various self-states that allow one to play "out of one's logical mind." If one is psychically dissociated, this self-state nonetheless remains embodied. A dissociated self-state has its own particular body and body performance. Playing "un-conscious" or in a different self-state where one does not know what one is doing implies that some part of the mind is not active. In fact, peak performance is never attained when you are thinking about it.

For instance, in my early days of playing, I was taught to try to visualize my tennis strokes. So I would close my eyes and imagine that my racquet was an extension of my arm. Even though my entire body would be tingling with excitement, I remained utterly relaxed and enjoyed every ball that whizzed toward me. Thinking I was absolutely sure that with my next stroke I could place the ball in any corner of my opponent's court, I visualized the court as enormously wide. That is how, in theory, I learned to block out my own distractions and was able to stay completely immersed in my own movements. I could maintain my ideal performance state. But why does this technique work only some of the time?

For many people, visualization benefits training by transforming complex motor procedures into automatic movements. Recently brain researchers have studied this phenomenon with imaging technologies. Stephen M. Kosslyn (2008) discovered that imagining a movement activates the same motor regions of the cerebral cortex that light up during the actual movement. Many researchers theorize that repeatedly visualizing the movement strengthens or adds synaptic connections among relevant neurons. And yet some studies indicate that breaking motion down into parts and concentrating on them in succession can hinder fluid coordination. The alternative is to imagine the outcome—not the motion, but its result.

I recently had my own experience with the positive effects of visualization. After watching Roger Federer win the Australian Open, I went out to play tennis myself and imagined that I was Federer. In my Federer-like self-state, I was impervious to the distractions that might disrupt my tennis capabilities. I "federized" my opponent and didn't experience the body arousal that typically affects my mental game. I was able to hit tennis shots that I know I am capable of but normally have trouble performing with any consistency. It was a great day—Federer won the Australian Open, and I was filled with excitement from having discovered a potential cure for my own head case. Sadly, though, within a week my Federer-self-state was gone.

Boundaries or infinite tennis

Like a rectangle with an infinite number of points inside it, tennis allows for an unlimited number of possibilities within the boundaries of the court. However, instead of thinking of tennis as a chaotic game that can be ordered into statistical facts (like the percentage of first serves in the box or the number of unforced errors), one could consider tennis as beginning with an ordered system of rules or structure that creates focused but inconceivably complex play that then becomes infinite (Wallace, 1996). One might say that the boundaries of tennis are like the boundaries of therapy, analysis, and supervision—in a sense, they create possibilities by limiting. Structure, by itself, however, is not enough. Tennis is structured well, but the goal that anchors it—winning—is arbitrary. One can be motivated to earn approval by succeeding in any sport, but, as with any sport, tennis is not enough to give meaning to one's life.

Courting Steve Mitchell

Keeping all this in mind, I reflect on an especially memorable tennis experience. In the late 1980s I was in my second year of analytic training at the William Alanson White Institute. This was the year of my supervision with Steve Mitchell. I was very fond of Steve as a person but was incredibly intimidated by his intellectual and clinical abilities. I would often leave our supervisory sessions feeling subpar and unable to engage his real interest in the case I was presenting. Knowing that Steve had a special appreciation for the psychoanalytic intellectual mind and realizing that I was coming from a far more eclectic background, I felt at a significant disadvantage. Still, I fought like a true competitor, desperate for his knowledge and yearning to become a "real" psychoanalyst. What, I wondered, would infuse life into this supervision?

With my first reference to tennis, I found the answer. I happily discerned that Steve's interest in my clinical case seemed to increase after I invited him to play tennis in my weekly doubles game on Monday nights at 10:00 p.m. (I note the time because, Steve, like a true tennis buff, was unfazed by the lateness of the court hour.) The mention of tennis infused life into the supervision as I experienced a level of involvement unseen so far in our clinical work. Questions bubbled over—what kind of racquet was I now playing with? What was the tension in my strings? Did I like the new synthetic gamma gut strings? Oh, I had played in college the first year of Title Nine? Oh???? What was it like being a ball girl for Bjorn Borg, Guillermo Vilas, Jimmy Connors in the US OPEN? ... and on ... and on.

For the first time I felt sparks of his unabashed interest and enthusiasm. I was eager to get him on the court and to have the opportunity playfully and maybe aggressively to be competitive in ways that I could not in the consulting room. Secretly I became aware of my desire to dominate and my hopes to try my hand at leveling our playing field. I felt I had nothing to lose by inviting Steve Mitchell to come play with us. I was curious to see what it would feel like to play against such a formidable intellectual opponent. I wondered what it would feel like to walk to the net (fighting the impulse to jump over it), shake Steve's hand, and say, "Good match!" with a win in hand. Or would I choke in the midst of the match, my thoughts focusing on the past, our supervision, or the future rather than on the present? Could I stay conscious of my emotional and physical reactions to this stressful but friendly game situation during the match? Or would I succumb to my "head case self-state"?

So I approached the tennis court in a sort-of "not-me" or unfamiliar aspect of my clinical dyad with Steve. I was cheerful, confident, and beaming with excitement. Steve, on the other hand, was nervously straining, reserved, and modestly present. I was hungry to engage with him and have him come and play on my turf (in my space). I wondered if, in the Winnicottian (1969) sense, I had to "destroy the object to find the object" (p. 712). We were expanding our interaction in a different physical space, where the limits of our emotions were less bounded by the confines of the supervisory relationship.

What I didn't know then but can know only now as I look back was that I was allowing myself—body and mind—to engage and experience the multitude of feelings within which I had felt imprisoned during our supervision. I freed myself up on the tennis court—my space—and, as a result, Steve freed up with me in our supervision—his space. Something happened through our interaction on the tennis court, a place where I felt I had nothing to lose. I felt more in my element on the court with Steve and went for it with everything I had. I could play in the zone and invest without overinvesting. I could gain access to my mind and body, and the result was smooth, fluid, and powerful strokes. Rather than falling into the pit, I could circle the demons and avoid the inner dissatisfaction, self-flagellation, and criticism that would otherwise have ensued. With each passing shot with Steve at the net and a few that I smashed right at him, I found myself feeling more relaxed. I gunned a heat-seeking missile right at him and found myself laughing. Could I be this aggressively playful in supervision, I wondered? It was my A game—all clutch saves without the choke. Steve, with utter graciousness, smiled at my tenacity and ferociousness, unseen until then in our supervision, and I felt the momentary victory of wanting and excelling and of Steve's acceptance of my being. My experience with Steve ignited in both of us intended acts that led to unintended consequences. Together we leveled the playing field both in tennis and in supervision—two similar kinds of play, after all.

It is a memory I will always cherish.

Tennis anyone? Advantage head case. Game. Set. Match.

Note

1 I would like to thank Ruth Livingston, Phillip Blumberg, Donnel Stern, Nick Samstag, and Philip Bromberg for their comments on earlier drafts of this paper and Irwin Hirsch for his invitation and remembering our original discussion.

References

Bromberg, P. (2009), Truth, human relatedness, and analytic process: An interpersonal/relational perspective. *International Journal of Psychoanalysis*, 90:347–361.

Crouse, K. (2009), Toss the ball. Hit the ball. Oops! Oops! *New York Times*, 9/1/09. p. A1.

Kosslyn, S. (2008), Using neuroimaging to resolve the psi debate. *Journal of Cognitive Neuroscience*, 20:182–192.

Wallace, D.F. (1996), *Infinite Jest*. New York: Little Brown.

Whitney, D., Wurnitsch, N., Hontiveros, B. & Louie, E. (2008), Perceptual mislocalization of bouncing balls by professional tennis referees. *Current Biology*, 18:R947–R948.

Winnicott, D.W. (1958), *Through Paediatrics to Psychoanalysis: Collected Papers*. New York: Brumer-Routledge, 1992.

Winnicott, D.W. (1969), The use of an object. *International Journal of Psychoanalysis*, 50:711–716.

A psychoanalytic look at sports fandom

Chapter 6

The faith of the fan

W. B. Carnochan, Ph.D.

The faith of the fan, when we seek to articulate it, is a labyrinth obscure as our faith in the visible world. The actions of fans are knowable. So, in some degree, are their states of mind. Experiments have demonstrated connections between the fortunes of fandom and activity in a remote tract of the brain, the ventral striatum, where risk is processed. But we'd like even more. The English word originated in the 17th century, then as now a jocular shortening of "fanatic," with religious overtones. Fanatics, in the eyes of the established church, were Protestant dissenters given to religious frenzies, speakers in tongues, holy rollers, "enthusiasts" of all stripes, those possessed by the gods. They appear, once as "Phans," once as "Fanns," in a hurly-burly text, mostly in verse, from the year 1682. A "fanatick," in Samuel Johnson's *Dictionary*, was "an enthusiast, a man mad with wild notions of religion." Madness, religious delirium, fever, disease—the Italian word is *tifoso*, from typhus—are the symptoms of fandom.

The modern lexical history of "fan" begins in journalism. In 1889 the *Kansas Times & Star* announced that "Kansas City baseball fans are glad they're through with Dave Rowe as a ball club manager," affording an otherwise unremembered player-manager of the Kansas City Cowboys a small place in lexical history. Soon the term worked its way sufficiently into the language, especially in newspapers, to appear in a list compiled by the Cornell University Dialect Society in 1902: "a baseball enthusiast; common among reporters." The first British usage was recorded in 1915, although still embraced in protective quotes (by the *Daily Express*): "First League football 'fans' in London can have a joyous time to-day."

But the flood tide was in full force: the world of baseball fans, fight fans, music fans, theater fans, even (in 1928) "League of Nations and disarmament fans," was quick to arrive. The word had been born again, as if to fill the spiritual needs of a new band of enthusiasts.

When Walter O'Malley took the Dodgers to Los Angeles in 1958, Brooklyn was torn by the grief, fury and despair of those abandoned by God. It was a dark night of the soul. Doris Kearns Goodwin (1977) was desolate, never to recover her faith in baseball until a friend took her to Boston's Fenway Park to see the Red Sox when she was a graduate student and she became attached to a new team. A familiar story has it that the journalist and novelist Pete Hamill and fellow journalist Jack Newfield decided after this ultimate act of treachery that the three most evil persons of the 20th century were, in order, Hitler, Stalin and Walter O'Malley (Newfield & Dunleavy, 2001). For some, the pain lingers. A poem of sorts is on the Web: "Against the game of baseball and the Brooklyn Dodgers' fan,/This crime had been committed by that foul O'Malley man." When O'Malley was admitted to baseball's Hall of Fame in 2007, almost 30 years after his death, the president of the Borough of Brooklyn said, "I'm flabbergasted ... A couple of weeks ago, I read that they were even considering honoring Walter O'Malley. I told them if they insisted on doing this, it would break the hearts of Brooklynites all over again." And "Never forgive, never forget," said Pete Hamill, still angry after nearly 50 years, although perhaps he boxed himself into his own persona: having ranked O'Malley the same as Hitler and Stalin, he would have had a moral problem if he had taken O'Malley's elevation to the Hall of Fame lying down.

But I took it calmly. After all, the Dodgers' World Series victory against the Yankees in 1955 had seemed to end a long and weary journey. And wasn't fandom a childish thing? Being a student seemed to coincide in its contours with the life, the ups-and-downs, of the fan, and I'd had enough of being a student. All the better, then, that living in the eastern time zone, three hours from Los Angeles, quieted nerves and dampened interest: the result of the previous night's game was not in the morning newspaper, the edge of anxiety was taken off. But when I drove to California to start a new life and heard Russ Hodges's voice on the car radio as I crossed the

Sierra, I felt the old hatreds rush back. A continent away, I still harbored the same world of feeling. The Dodgers were the Dodgers, whether in Brooklyn or in Los Angeles. Dodger-hood (call it) survived—and still does, even though, in the intervening years, the stability of every baseball franchise has been tested by new rules of free agency: players move from team to team in a never-ending dance of dollars. Throughout the 1970s, the Dodger infield consisted of Steve Garvey at first, Davey Lopes at second, Bill Russell at shortstop, and Ron Cey at third. That sort of stability no longer happens: no four infielders would play the same position for the same club over 10 years. Yet the Dodgers still keep their identity. True, we can imagine circumstances when they might not. Suppose they moved to Arkansas and became the Little Rock Dodgers. Suppose their Little Rock roster had no players from the previous year in Los Angeles. The Little Rock Dodgers would not be my Dodgers. Dodgerhood would be dead. Or would it? We're in the territory of Heraclitus, Parmenides, Plato—and God, the unchanging changer.

At the end of Goodwin's (1977) *Wait Till Next Year* the publisher offers a "discussion point" for book club readers that brings up Goodwin's Catholic girlhood:

> Doris's careful calculations of baseball scores and batting averages charmingly mirror the manner in which she tallies up her nightly prayers. Discuss the mingled roles of baseball and religion in Doris's childhood. Was baseball a kind of secular worship for her?
>
> (p. 268)

How to answer that last question? Yes? No? But what is true beyond doubt, sports in general, perhaps baseball in particular, elicits attitudes, behaviors, and beliefs that make an association with religion seem natural. Not only does "fan" have its remote origin in the fanatic enthusiasm of 17th-century sects, Ranters and Diggers, Fifth Monarchy Men and Muggletonians; not only do we make demigods of the great Dodger pitcher, Sandy Koufax, and (for me) the most wonderful of tennis players, Roger Federer; not only did David Foster Wallace (2006) once describe watching Federer as a "bloody near-religious experience"—a near-religious experience marked, I'd add, by anxiety amounting to near-religious terror—in the Wimbledon finals of 2007, 2008, and 2009—but the behavior of fans, like that of players, is notable for its magical rituals, call them compulsive or prayerful, either will do. The magical practices of players have even drawn academic attention. *Conformity and Conflict* (Spradley & McCurdy, 1996), a collection of readings in cultural anthropology, includes a study of "baseball magic" by George Gmelch (1977) sandwiched between magic and religion in New Guinea on one side and Satanism in San Francisco on the other. The study tallies up an extraordinary number of players' rituals, taboos, and fetishes. Among the rituals: one pitcher, after every pitch, would "reach into his back pocket to touch a crucifix, straighten his cap and clutch his genitals" (p. 421). Another: before a game, sanding varnish off a bat, then rubbing rosin into the grain and heating the bat over a flame, a witches' brew of double, double, toil and trouble, which prompted one informant to tell George Gmelch, not only a student of baseball but a former minor leaguer, "There may not be a God, but I go to church just the same" (p. 423). Among the taboos: not mentioning a no-hitter in progress, the taboo that Red Barber broke so fearlessly in the World Series of 1947—and thereby, some might think, wrecked Floyd Bevens's chance at baseball immortality. Among the fetishes: practically anything from old shoes to hairpins. Gmelch observes, following Bronislaw Malinowski, that ritual magic is a tactic useful in situations of great uncertainty. In a game when batters get hits about 25% of the time, uncertainty hangs heavy on every pitch.

Fans exercise their own sorcery. When she was seven years old, Doris Kearns Goodwin made her first confession with a heavy conscience: she had to report that she had gone to an Episcopal church to see the fine (and warm-hearted) Dodger catcher Roy Campanella, she had talked in church, been disobedient, wished harm to others, talked back to her teacher. The priest, having a good sense of priorities, seized on the lone revelation that, from a seven-year-old, would raise an eyebrow. To whom, he asked, had Doris wished harm? The answer: any number of ballplayers who weren't Dodgers. She hoped Allie Reynolds, the Yankee pitcher, would break his arm; that Phil Rizzuto would fracture his rib; that Richie Ashburn of the Phillies would break his hand. This is a sophisticated reconstruction of a seven-year-old's feelings—but the burden of it is real. Magical imagining of harm to an enemy makes part of the fan's everyday experience.

Goodwin's black magic was no doubt balanced by the spells of others working the other side. Fans' white magic is as frequent as its dark counterpart. David Halberstam (2006) tells a story of his friend Joe Lelyveld, later executive editor of the *New York Times*, but then a sixth grader and diehard Yankee fan. His youthful rituals—bouncing a ball against a wall, staring out the window of his Upper West Side apartment at an advertising sign across the river, focusing ever more intently on the sign at crucial moments—were white magic on behalf of Tommy Henrich, then the Yankees' most reliable hitter while Joe DiMaggio was out early in the season with an injury. And the magic worked. In 1987 Halberstam and Lelyveld met at a party. When Halberstam said he was writing a book about the Yankees and Red Sox in summer, 1949, Lelyveld asked slyly if he knew about Henrich's 15 or so important home runs while DiMaggio was out of action. Halberstam said, "I knew that, but how the hell did *you* know that?" Lelyveld's answer (of course): "I helped him do it" (p. 319). As a child of much the same age, I used to toss a tennis ball endlessly against the wall in my Manhattan apartment, often with the Dodgers on the radio. The shadow of the late afternoon sun cut across the wall. My target was the angle between sun and shadow. I helped the Dodgers win some games.

Near the end of Nick Hornby's (1988) *Fever Pitch*, a story of one fan's obsession, the narrator contemplates his unending, once youthful attachment to the English football club Arsenal: "I can no longer use age, or rather youth, to explain myself in the way I have been able to do elsewhere." Others will not make the allowances they used to: "As I get older, the tyranny that football exerts over my life, and therefore over the lives of people around me, is less reasonable and less attractive" (p. 205). Put away childish things, we're told; stop aiming that tennis ball at the line between sun and shadow. Yet there would be a cost, and the same Scripture that tells us to put away childish things also tells us to keep the faith. Hornby could have ended *Fever Pitch* with a goodbye to all this, but he does not. Conceding the mysterious tyranny of football that obstructs his ordinary life, and remembering the horror that befell a football crowd in 1989 when almost 100 people died in a crush, he wonders how he managed to attend and enjoy a football match 16 days after the disaster. The answer: "Nothing ever matters, apart from football" (p. 217). The excesses of fandom would make good material for a religious taxonomy such as William James attempted, except that psychology, like baseball, has been taken over by numbers: instead of James's distinction between healthy minds and sick souls, scalar measurement would do the job now, a one-to-seven scale, for example, with zero interest at the low end and unrelenting fanaticism at the high end. The serious fan, whether at seven on the scale (Hornby, probably) or six (I, probably, although my friend Paul Alpers, an astute reader, detects a decline down the scale to five), will not be deterred by stadium disasters or an imperative to grow up. Waving a final, casual farewell to the Dodgers as they packed their bags to Los Angeles was just an idle hope. After the stadium disaster Hornby does not do the grown-up thing and put madness aside. Instead we hear of Arsenal's greatest triumph, a stunning victory over Liverpool, May 26, 1989, to win the Championship League, "the greatest moment ever" (p. 217), says Hornby's narrator. The idea that Arsenal could win the Championship after years of frustration, like the idea that the Brooklyn Dodgers would ever win the World Series, required faith—it was "something you either believe in or you don't, like God" (p. 218)—a faith sorely tested but eventually repaid. God doesn't like backsliders: "Thy backslidings shall reprove thee" (Jeremiah 2. 19). Or: "Return, ye backsliding children, and I will heal your backslidings" (Jeremiah 3. 22). True fans keep the faith.

References

Gmelch, G. J. (1977), Baseball Magic. In: *Conformity and Conflict: Readings in Cultural Anthropology*, ed. J.P. Spradley & D.W. McCurdy. New York: Little, Brown, pp. 310–319, 1996.
Goodwin, D.K. (1977), *Wait Till Next Year*. New York: Simon & Schuster.
Halberstam, D. (2006), *Summer of '49*. New York: Harper Perennial Modern Classics.
Hornby, N. (1988), *Fever Pitch*. New York: Riverhead Books.
Newfield, J. & Dunleavy, S. (2001), Scribes recreate bar scene. www.nypost.com/p/news/scribes_recreate_bar_scene_YonX2S5HQ5c5EePU66x64.

Spradley, J. & McCurdy, D.W. eds. (1996), *Conformity and Conflict: Readings in Cultural Anthropology.* New York: Little, Brown.

Wallace, D. F. (2006), Federerer as religous experience. www.nytimes.com/2006/08/20/sports/playmagazine/20federer.html?_r=1.

Chapter 7

A relational view of passion in sports and the group experience[*]

Robert I. Watson, Jr., Ph.D.

Passion, defined as "a feeling by which the mind is powerfully affected" (Oxford, 1971), is evident in many group experiences and behaviors. One can speak of passion experienced and demonstrated in the group setting and one can speak of passion for the group itself. There can also be the shared passion within the group focused on someone or something outside the group. The positive emotional meaning of passion is evident in the intense experiences often seen at sporting events. Passion for the sport is one aspect of these emotional reactions. As Hemingway (1926) stated in *The Sun Also Rises*, "Aficion means passion. An aficionado is one who is passionate about bullfighting" (p. 136). Hemingway is also contrasting true lovers of the sport from those who are only interested. One can find groups of like-minded lovers of many other experiences, from ballet and opera to stamp collecting. The simple reality of the object is not what draws the individuals together; it is the emotional experience associated with it. In many cases it is also the active experience of taking part with others in the sharing of knowledge of the loved object. The defining group experience is the passion for the object and the shared experience of this passion. Passion is not always directed at a sport in general but can be focused on a group, the "team," that the "fan" has a connection to and often admires. An excellent example of this form of passion is found in Salman Rushdie's description of his relationship to an English football club, the Tottenham Hotspur, which is also my favorite team (1999). He recounts his original attraction to the team and writes with great passion about his thoughts, feelings, and relationship to the team throughout the years.

The display of this passion is most readily seen at large sporting events. "Sports evoke strong passions: awe and elation, depression and disgust, omnipotence and humiliation, grief and despair" (Seligman, 2010, p. 562). Fans come together to watch their teams, but also to enjoy the group experience with like-minded individuals. The setting allows and encourages passionate emotional displays from individuals and the group. This is especially evident with men who would not allow themselves to express strong emotions in most social interactions, but in a group of fans allow themselves to be highly emotional, yelling, screaming, even hugging others.

Carnochan (2010) points out the word "fan" itself is an abbreviation of the word "fanatic," which clearly has religious overtones and speaks to the emotional devotion and faith sports fans can experience for their teams. Bonding with other fans can take on an almost ritualized aspect, as with the team songs at Premier League Football matches. Insider aspects of the fan group experiences often happen within the group context, leading to further bonding among the group members. At most NY Rangers hockey games, a fan will whistle a few bars and the fans will yell in unison "Potvin sucks," deprecating a rival star player of the 1980s. This action demonstrates knowledge of the team and is another aspect of group bonding. These passionate displays lead to greater identification with the team and greater identification with the group that shares the emotional experience. Passion both helps build bonds between group members and leads to greater identification with the group itself.

Many men and women identify themselves as an athlete, especially in adolescence and early adulthood. As one grows older, some individuals maintain a self concept as an athlete, but for many there is a change of focus to being a fan, and often a fan of the sport they took part in earlier. Their passion for playing the sport changes to a passion for watching the sport. This different, though related, self concept can become an important aspect of an individual's self system.

Positive emotions are our usual associations with passion. There is, however, an older meaning of passion–suffering, "the experience of a powerful affliction or disorder" (Oxford, 1971). Passion with this definition can also be a unifier of the individual with the group and the group can aid in the expression of these negative emotions. Bonding with the group can be experienced around the painful emotion and the group can be an outlet for the open expression of the negative passion. Again, evidence for this can be seen in sport. As ABC Wide World of Sports' tag line said, athletes experience both the "Thrill of Victory" and the "Agony of Defeat." Athletes can experience negative passion in defeat, whether they are part of a team or involved in an individual sport. The team and group experience aids both in the expression and containment of emotions. Also the expression of a negative passion and interactions between team members around this passion can lead to greater bonding in the team. Witness the greater team effort of the NY Rangers in 2014 after the death of Martin St. Louis' mother and his returning to the team, speaking openly about his loss. The experience of fans of a team in a group after an important defeat can be helpful for the fans in more openly expressing their disappointment and sadness and can aid in both containing the experience and in bonding among the fan group.

There is a cycle of passion in many group situations. The group setting gives many individuals the ability to release passion more openly. This experience of expression then leads to more bonding and identification with the group. This, in turn, leads to greater group cohesiveness, which can lead to passion being more easily experienced and expressed in the group.

There are many individual and relational factors that lead to this cycle of passion in the group. One area that is important to consider is the strength of the individual's ego identity and their need to be attached to a group. As Ron Aviram (2009) has pointed out in his relational book on prejudice, some individuals with weaker ego identities need to be attached and identified with an "in group." This can happen with team members and fans of a team. I think a second factor can play an even more important role and that is the flexibility in an individual's ego identity that can allow the person to be passionate in the group setting. This in turn suggests a shift in self states that can be a strength and a sign of flexibility in the individual (Bromberg, 1996). The group setting can be conducive for the individual to experience this change in self state and help him to be more open emotionally. The group experience, by allowing passion, leads to greater bonding and identification with the group.

It is also important to consider that this passionate experience in the group is being carried out within the context of "play," whether one is watching or participating in the sport. Play in itself is a very important aspect of our psychological life, and sports is one way many have to integrate it into one's life. Building on Winnicott (1971), Greif (2010) states:

> Sports, games, and intense bodily pursuits ... enable us to rediscover and retain our connection to an essential source of creativity and vitality, one which we may always be vulnerable to losing touch.
>
> (p. 560)

Therefore, the expression of passion within this context of play can have a very important effect on the individual and their psychological wellbeing.

There are, of course, many factors that are not intersubjective nor strictly relational that lead a person to identify with a group. Again, in sports, one sees the impact of neighborhood and family on one's identification with a team. Location of one's home certainly plays an important role, whether it be for which horse to cheer for at the Palio in Siena or which football team to support in Manchester. Family history with a team can be very important in leading to support and identification with a team. One's choice can also be a statement of rebellion within the family when the preferred team is rejected. Identification and passion for a team also has interesting developmental factors as possible reasons for the attachment to the team. Recently an economist did a study on how childhood experiences could shape an individual's team preferences (Stephens-Davidowitz, 2014). Using data from Facebook, he was able to determine the degree of passion one has for a major league baseball team. After controlling for numerous factors, the most important element determining one's degree of "fandom" was the team winning a championship during the adult's childhood years, specifically eight or nine years old for adult men. Winning a World Series when a boy is eight years old increases the chance he will support that team as an adult by 8%. This passion for the team factor is much less if the championship is won when the boy is 14 or older. As an economist the author does not offer any psychological reason for these findings. From an interpersonal perspective, it is interesting to note that this age range falls squarely in Harry Stack Sullivan's (1953) juvenile era. In Sullivan's estimation this was a period of development when the child is beginning to look outside the family for relationships and identifications and experiences competitiveness. The years around eight or nine could certainly be a time for the boy to identify with a strong winning group, and for this passion and identification to carry into adulthood.

Passion is an important aspect of many group settings. It is also important in the "healing" process that we strive for in psychotherapy groups. Group psychotherapy has many elements to it that aid the healing process for the individual. As Yalom (1975) has emphasized in his classic work on group psychotherapy, just as the relationship is paramount in individual treatment, group cohesiveness is primary in group psychotherapy. Passion, with both meanings, can be a major force in group cohesion. It is in the sharing of passion that the group coheres, then focuses on working through and understanding these emotions for the individual patient.

Bion's (1970) concept of containment is also useful in explaining the power of groups in aiding the therapeutic process. When there is an expression of passion in the group and there is an acceptance of it, the strong emotions are contained in the group. This Bion (1962) has suggested is akin to the mother being able to contain and mirror her infant's emotions. In the therapy group this containment can lead to therapeutic gain for both the individual with the passion and the other group members who are able to reflect and contain the emotions. It is in this interplay between the container and the contained that much of the relational work of the group is carried out.

Passion also affects the group leader. As Billow (2003) pointed out in his book on relational group psychotherapy, the role of the group leader is paramount in helping the group reach its therapeutic goals. He or she must join the group in its passionate interactions but also maintain and assert a separate point of view. The group leader must be aware of such phenomena as projective identification, their own experience of bonding with the group members and their own countertransference. Observing and facilitating both verbal and nonverbal aspects of bonding can greatly aid in group cohesiveness and eventually identification with the group.

Passion for Bion (1963) has a very specific meaning and is in many ways the ultimate goal of the group process. By passion he meant an integrated intersubjective sensibility which takes place within the group setting. This comes about in the group when what he terms the primal affects, Love, Hate and Knowing, are brought into awareness as feelings and thoughts in the group. I agree that this is an important goal of group psychotherapy, but I also believe passion defined in the two more common definitions is important in understanding group process. Passion relates to the group cohesiveness and the bonding process in the group. Containment of the passion of an individual in the group leads to better understanding of it and to greater bonding among the group members.

There is one more relational factor that is important to take into account with passion and the healing process within the group. This is the concept of individual identity and the need for identification with the group. As with fans' identification with their group, a group setting can aid in the expression of passion for an individual. In a therapeutic group passion can be more easily expressed by some individuals because their identification with the group helps them overcome their inhibitions for emotional expression (Yalom, 1975). Conversely, identification with the group can aid in containing the emotions in the group so they do not have to be acted on outside the therapeutic setting. The group setting can also lead to the individual losing some of the rigidity of self states and can lead to attempting new forms of interaction in the group, which in turn can lead to flexibility in self states (Bromberg, 1996). For example, the group member who begins to reach out and help other group members rather than having a self focus can begin to be more flexible in their interactions inside and outside of group and begin to experience their self in new ways. One of the most rigid self states that I have encountered is the Depressive Self and this has been a major focus of my work in groups.

My clinical experience with group psychotherapy has been at the Columbia Doctor's Day Treatment Program, an intensive outpatient group program for high functioning individuals, most of whom are depressed or bipolar. All patients have an outside psychotherapist, often a psychopharmacologist, and often come to the program after a hospitalization. There are both dynamic and structured psychotherapy groups. Most patients attend the program from 4 to 9 months and attend 4 to 10 groups a week.

Passion aids the process of the groups in a variety of ways. The factors of group focus and the expression of negative passion in the group are the greatest aids in the healing process and therapeutic outcome. With teams and fans the passionate focus of the group is centered on winning. In these psychotherapy groups the focus is on recovery and return to functioning of the group members. The passion here is in defeating depression and moving toward a more functional life. The depression/agony, the negative passion, is explored by individuals in the relative safety and empathy of the group. These two factors have great agency in moving patients away from depression. By speaking about their depression the group members begin to bond with the others in the group. This experience can in turn lead to a containment of the negative passion in the group. This is especially important in dealing with suicidal ideation, which is often expressed by patients in the day treatment program. Recently, my older adult dynamic group dealt with a member having strong suicidal ideation. She had been a group member for 7 weeks and had taken an active role in group discussions. She spoke in depth about her depressive feelings and her tentative plan to kill herself. The group reacted by reaching out empathically to her since many had experienced suicidal ideation in the past. They helped her explore both internal and external triggers for her present emotional state. There were attempts at understanding and explanation but no panic or rejection in the group members' interactions with her. One member was even able to help her make connections to past traumas in her life. Overall, she was able to express and experience the agony of depression in the group and found it could be contained in the group.

An added factor to the success of containment of passion in the group is that the group can be experienced as a safe place to "play" with interpersonal relations. Winnicott (1971) has emphasized the role of "play" in individual treatment, but it can also be a major factor in the therapeutic effectiveness of the group. The group can aid the patient in expressing and experiencing new forms of passion and new self systems. The freedom to play within the group can lead to a demystification of one's pattern of emotional interactions and can then help with therapeutic change for the individual. For example, at one time a number of younger adult patients were introduced as new group members to an established group that had a number of patients who were 20 years older. One younger patient had an immediate reaction to the older patients, becoming emotionally dysregulated and verbally attacking them. On reflection the patient was able to see how she had played out a transference reaction with the older patients and was able to understand and comment on her anger in a useful manner. She was then able to work with the older group members and began to understand how similar emotional reactions had affected her professional life. The group setting aided in her expressing and playing with her emotional reactions and helped her contain and better understand these reactions.

Passion in terms of the group focus is also very important in the therapeutic effectiveness of the day-program groups. With the focus of the group on becoming less depressed and being more able to function at work and socially, many patients feel supported in the changes they attempt to make in their behavior and in their self states.

One example of this change in self states and behavior was evident in a patient who worked both in the dynamic and structured groups. He was a successful engineer for high tech firms. He had struggled with depression for most of his life, and at 45 became extremely depressed, isolating himself, being unable to work and not feeling able to carry out most physical activities. In the dynamic groups he was accepted as another person suffering with depression and was encouraged to express his feelings about the depression, his frustration about not working, and his loneliness. In the structured depressive management group he was encouraged to be more active and focus on lifestyle issues such as eating properly and exercise. The group also asked him to speak about his most depressive and self-torturing thoughts and to challenge them with more positive thoughts in the group. He worked in both the dynamic and structured groups and slowly began to change, contacting old friends and making initial phone calls to his principle high tech firm. In both forms of group he would speak about his depression and often not see any of the gains he had made. The groups helped him see and accept the changes he was able to make. He also began to empathically make comments to the other patients, using a self system he had not been able to use in a long time, helping many of them with their struggles. Through these interactions he bonded with the group members and began to identify with the group. He then became more able to use the group as a container for many of his negative passions. The containment in turn allowed him to experience more positive passion and to free himself from some aspects of his depressive self. A primary factor in his recovery was the focus on the passion to change in both forms of group. He built on this passion and was able to become functional in both work and relationships.

Passion plays a role in many group experiences, whether it be at a sporting event or in a psychotherapy group. Passion both bonds the individuals together and leads to greater group identification, which in turn can lead to more emotional expression of passion. The containment in the group can help the individual with the passion and in itself can be healing. This interaction with passion works well within groups that are dedicated to the reduction of the negative passion of depression, and therefore passion can have a central role in healing within the group process.

Note

* An earlier version of this chapter appeared as A relational view of passion and the group experience. In (2018) B. Willock, R. Curtis and L. Bohm (Eds.) *Psychoanaltic Perspectives on Passion.* (pp. 210–216). London: Routledge.

References

Aviram, R. B. (2009). *The Relational Origin of Prejudice.* Lanham, NY: Jason Aronson.
Billow, R. M. (2003). *Relational Group Psychotherapy.* London: Jessica Kingsley.
Bion, W. R. (1962). *Learning from Experience.* London: Heinemann.
Bion, W. R. (1963). *Elements of Psycho-analysis.* London: Heinemann.
Bion, W. R. (1970). *Attention and Interpretation.* London: Tavistock.

Bromberg, P. M. (1996). Standing in the spaces: the multipilicity of self and the psychoanalytic relationship. *Contemporary Psychoanalysis*, 32: 509–535.

Carnochan, W. B. (2010). The faith of the fan. *Contemporary Psychoanalysis*, 46: 504–509.

Greif, D. (2010). Revaluing sports. *Contemporary Psychoanalysis*, 46: 550–561.

Hemingway, E. (1926). *The Sun Also Rises*. New York: Scribner.

Oxford English Dictionary, Compact Edition. (1971). Glasgow: Oxford University Press.

Rushdie, S. (1999). The people's game. *The New Yorker*. May 31.

Seligman, S. (2010). The sensibility of baseball. *Contemporary Psychoanalysis*, 46: 562–577.

Stephens-Davidowitz, S. (2014). They hook you when you're young. *The New York Times*. April 20.

Sullivan, H.S. (1953). *The Interpersonal Theory of Psychiatry*. New York: Norton.

Winnicott, D. W. (1971). *Playing and Reality*. New York: Routledge.

Yalom, I. D. (1975). *The Theory and Practice of Group Psychotherapy*. New York: Basic Books.

Chapter 8

Sports—applied psychoanalysis
Par excellence

James Hansell, Ph.D.

A quick visit to Amazon.com, or perusal of the local newspaper sports page, seems to support the contention that sports bring out the best and the worst in human nature. Consider the following examples.

After yet another win, coach Roger Barta, of the record-setting Smith Center, Kansas high school varsity football team, tells his boys,

> When you go home tonight, I want you to tell your parents you love them for all they do for you. They are there for you guys, and that is what life is all about. In fact, if we in this room are there for each other every day this season, we'll all be part of something special.
>
> (Drape, 2009a)

Coach Barta tells Drape (also the author of *Our Boys: A Perfect Season on the Plains with the Smith Center Redman*, 2009b), "You know this isn't about football, this is about raising kids. It's what we do really well here, and it's what we're proud of."

But just a few clicks away, one finds very different books and news stories. In a *New York Times* review of André Agassi's autobiography *Open*, the reviewer recounts how Agassi's father, Mike, "subjected all four of his children to abusive training, yanking them out of school for extra practice time. The three eldest all crumbled under the pressure" (Tanenhaus, 2009). During the same week that Agassi's book was reviewed, a YouTube video of University of New Mexico soccer player Elizabeth Lambert violently attacking an opposing player became an Internet sensation.

Stories like these are part of the beat of Mark Hyman, also a reporter for the *New York Times* and author of *Until It Hurts: America's Obsession with Youth Sports and How It Harms Our Kids* (2009). Hyman focuses on the out-of-control extremes of contemporary youth sports in America. Alongside his extensive documentation of the exploitation of athletes at all levels, Hyman describes, in painful detail, his own complicity in pushing his son to overuse his pitching arm to the point that the teenager required "Tommy John" surgery to continue competing.[1]

How are we to understand these contrasting extremes? What is it about sports that elicits honor, love, and fellowship, on one hand, and narcissism, cheating, exploitation, and violence, on the other? How, for that matter, can we understand the depth of passion that so many people feel about sports—to the point that sports can become very much like an addiction, as Nick Hornby (1998) so poignantly portrays in *Fever Pitch*, his memoir of growing up obsessed with the Arsenal soccer club? What accounts for most children's natural love of sports, and the importance it seems to play in childhood and adolescent development? Do quaint ideas about sports as a crucial venue for learning about teamwork, the "importance of disappointment" (Craib, 1994), and other life lessons still apply? If sports are so important to the development of young people, how are nonathletic children affected? What was missed by the generations of girls who had few athletic outlets before the relatively recent explosion of athletic opportunities for women?

At the interpersonal level, what is going on when parents and fans treat athletes like commodities, to be enjoyed, controlled, and marketed? We hear a great deal today about "helicopter" parents of all varieties, including the overidentified, pushy sports parent, intent on getting his or her child that vaunted college athletic scholarship. Is this a truly new phenomenon or just a current version of age-old "stage parenting"? In professional sports, many additional factors come into play and sport is pushed to extremes. "We want to see excess, we want to see the contest taken to the ultimate limit and we are willing to pay handsomely for it. Our demand for winning is what drives much of the excess in the sports world today," writes Stefan Szymanski (2009). But why are sports such an intense, ubiquitous, and enduring social and cultural practice? How do sports relate to social conflict and cohesion, to military and religious structures? Does the supposed claim by Arthur Wellesley that "[t]he battle of

Waterloo was won on the playing fields of Eton" have any contemporary, or for that matter, historical truthfulness?

My argument here is that answers to these questions concerning sports *require* a "depth" psychology like psychoanalysis. Many readers seem to balk (no pun intended) at encountering the words psychoanalysis and sports in the same sentence. The origins of this split may harken back to high school, when teens who were interested in sports and those who were interested in weighty matters such as psychoanalysis seemed to live in different universes.

Fortunately, we are no longer in high school, and thus we have an opportunity to reflect on the relationships between sport and psychoanalysis. These relationships are multiple and profound. Indeed, I have come to believe that sports is a psychoanalytic topic *par excellence*, a poster child for "applied psychoanalysis" (and thereby also a terrific teaching tool). Indeed, a number of specific psychoanalytic theories are uniquely positioned to illuminate the examples with which I opened this essay and other similar athletic phenomena. Sports exemplify Freudian basic concepts such as unconscious motivation, unconscious conflict and compromise, and the centrality of sexual, aggressive, narcissistic, and attachment themes throughout the human life cycle (Freud, 1933). Sports also provide powerful illustrations of some of the important recent developments in psychoanalytic theory, including Lacan's (1949) work on the Imaginary and Symbolic registers; Kohut's (1977) psychology of the self and the role of self objects in development; Butler's (1990) feminist psychoanalytic theories on performativity, gender binaries, and the unmourned losses at the root of gender; Laplanche's (1989) "general theory of seduction"; and even the work of the psychoanalytically influenced sociologist René Girard (1979), I touch on each of these authors later. Finally, sports has a natural kinship with psychoanalysis because both involve the interrelationships among the intrapsychic, interpersonal, and social realms. While arguing primarily that sports are a unique and inviting canvas for the expression of psychodynamic forces—much like a "dream screen"—I also secondarily propose that the dynamics involved in our passion for sports and for athletes is, in some respects, a displacement from other concerns and conflicts. In particular, some of the current critiques of sport in America, such as Hyman's (2009) work, represent a kind of hysterical cultural symptom in which deeper intrapsychic, interpersonal, and social conflicts are disguised by pointing "over there" at sports.

Sports and the intrapsychic

In Lacanian terms, sport immerses us in the world of the Imaginary—the world of idealizations, illusions, and all-encompassing binaries (Lacan, 1949). In professional sports, the *process* of playing matters only as it affects the *outcome*, as Vince Lombardi famously stated in proclaiming that "winning isn't the most important thing; it's the *only* thing." Sports, with their emphasis on the win–lose binary and on the idealization of the athletic body, highlight the longing to be (or in the case of the fan, to be identified with) the biggest, the strongest, and the fastest. Is there any better example of the universal obsession with the Lacanian Phallus than sports? Think of the visceral rush that occurs when we watch LeBron James's grace and power as he completes a thundering dunk. Or the feeling of awe in watching Derek Jeter, in tradition-laden Yankee pinstripes, making an impossible play. Or the joy in seeing Serena Williams smash an opponent's misplaced lob.

In this sense, sport implicates the athlete and the fan in reliving two crucial developmental phases—Lacan's (1949) mirror phase, in which subjectivity is first formed, and adolescence, the phase during which the tension between the Imaginary to the Symbolic registers is powerfully revisited. When fans view their favorite players as idealized figures and experience each win or loss with extreme emotional changes accompanied by fluctuating serotonin and testosterone levels, they are exemplifying the Lacanian subject who reifies and concretizes the illusion of wholeness, perfection, and mastery in signifiers like "champion," "all star," and "winner." Similarly, when parents and coaches push young athletes to succeed in order to meet their own narcissistic needs, they are mistaking the child for the Phallus, and the Phallus for themselves.

By contrast, Coach Barta (and others with similar perspectives) demonstrates the potential that sports can also be experienced at the Symbolic level, as (serious) *play* rather than concretized and fetishized. In this more mature mode, sports can be a venue for connectedness and need, and for learning to live with imperfection, rather than a pursuit of perfection and a corresponding *denial* of human "lack," incompleteness, and interdependence.

In a very specific link between psychoanalysis and sports at the intrapsychic level, sports are also the venue for many of the most profound processes in gender identity development and maintenance. Judith Butler's (1990) work on gender performativity and on melancholic gender identity structures is particularly helpful in understanding this aspect of sports. For example, sports are often an arena of gender "performance" in the sense that Butler describes. Less obvious is the way sports serve to protect, while simultaneously disguising, the "unmourned" homoerotic ties from early childhood that must be disavowed in a heteronormative culture. This includes, but also goes beyond, the observation that for many men sports provide acceptable cover for having an emotional life that would otherwise seem dangerously feminine or gay. In addition, playing sports with same-sex peers, or enjoying sports as an aspect of "male bonding," can serve as a compromise formation in which forbidden states and longings, including homoerotic closeness to other men, are sublimated and made acceptable to the psyche by being saturated in the masculine matrix of sport (see Hirsch, 1999).

Interestingly, the other side of this coin is that sports can also provide opportunities for the expansion of gender identity, for reconnection with lost aspects of the self, and for non-melancholic identity structures. Consider, again, Coach Barta and the Smith Center Redmen. By providing "feminine" nurturance along with "fatherly" guidance from male mentors, Coach Barta and his staff intuitively made it safe for the young men to accept and even embrace, rather than reject, their "feminine" traits of loving and supporting their families and teammates. This example perfectly mirrors Diamond's (2008) theorizing regarding the role of the available, nurturant father in helping young boys develop secure gender identity without excessive reliance on the normative forms of splitting (i.e., gender binaries) that typically provide the defensive structures around which gender conflicts are consolidated.

Sports and the interpersonal/relational

I have already alluded to the interpersonal dimension of sports fan-dom in terms of Lacanian concepts such as the Phallus and the Imaginary register—the use of the athlete, team, or athletic prowess to maintain narcissistic identity illusions. Other theorists, of course, have developed this line of thinking further into the interpersonal realm than Lacan. For me, the work of Laplanche (1989), particularly his "general theory of seduction," is very helpful in understanding such "proxy" relationships.

Laplanche has explored the tension between endogenous and exogenous models of desire in psychoanalysis—desire as originating in the self (e.g., the Freudian conception of the id) versus desire as a product of the desire of the Other. Laplanche's general theory of seduction, picked up by Greenberg (2001), Harris (2009), and others, offers a radical figure–ground reversal of the Freudian picture. It suggests that far more radical and disturbing than the discovery of the unconscious per se is the idea that the unconscious is molded by the unarticulated desire of the Other (in this case, the primary caretakers), unlike Freud's drive-based id. Laplanche's (somewhat misleadingly named) general theory of seduction is, of course, highly influenced by Lacan's views on language and the Unconscious as the discourse of the Other, but Laplanche adds developmental specificity. In particular, Laplanche argues that most identity pathologies result from "enigmatic," unconsciously transmitted sexual messages from the adult/parent imposed on the child—a kind of confusion of tongues (Ferenczi, 1933). In this view, the "bedrock" traumas involved in identity formation have much less to do with endogenous factors like oedipal conflicts, or with exogenous cultural factors like the Law of the Father or compulsory heterosexuality, than they do with exogenous factors closer to home—the child's difficulty managing enigmatic pressures from within the family.

Applied to phenomena like "stage parenting" and athletic versions thereof, Laplanche's (1989) theory of seduction provides theoretical scaffolding for understanding the effects of such parenting on a child. In its "healthy" variant, the parent's desire for the child—in this case, desire for the child to be a certain kind of athlete—is relatively unconflicted for the parent; hence, the pressures are expressed openly rather than "enigmatically." In addition, the parent's desire for the child, with which the child identifies, fits reasonably well with the child's capacities and temperamental tendencies. Finally, the parent has sufficient mastery over his or her desires to be able to maintain a reasonable balance between the needs of the adult and the needs of the child.

Clinical experience and extensive observation (admittedly anecdotal) suggest that the foregoing conditions may be more the exception than the rule. More commonly, the desire of the parent in the arena of athletic performance is imbued with considerable narcissistic, sexual, and aggressive conflict, resulting in the kind of enigmatic transmission and pressures described by Laplanche. Furthermore, the parent's unresolved conflicts, which are expressed in identity expectations and pressures on the child, are not necessarily in synchrony with the child's developmental needs nor sufficiently differentiated from the child. An important related phenomenon is unconscious parental guilt about this psychological "use" of the child. This is a subject covered up by powerful, but largely unrecognized, taboos, and it emerges mainly in displaced and disguised forms. When it is addressed directly (as in Jane Smiley's, 1990, remarkable short story "Ordinary Love" about a woman's confrontation with the psychological damage she has done to her children) one has the sense that it can still only be glanced at briefly. (I have more to say about this later when discussing the cultural dynamics of sport.) On rare occasions, parents and coaches will be consciously aware of these dynamics and be able to tolerate the guilt, painful though it is. Mark Hyman's (2009) account of his culpability in his son's arm overuse and subsequent surgery is a poignant example.

Sports and culture

It is frequently said that sports are "tribal," or a substitute for warfare, and there is considerable truth in these statements. But what do these statements really mean, and how can we understand the processes involved?

In this context, the work of René Girard (1979), the psychoanalytically informed sociologist and philosopher, offers some helpful concepts, particularly those regarding "mimetic rivalry" and "scapegoating." In brief, Girard argues that human desire is fundamentally *mimetic*, or imitative (an important concept itself for understanding the contagious qualities of sports fan-dom). For Girard, the importance of the mimetic structure of desire is that it inevitably leads to conflict and potential violence, since people end up desiring the same things and cannot all have them. Societies find different ways of managing these tensions, some quite destructive and others relatively constructive. Girard views "scapegoating" as one of the more primitive and destructive, but widespread, social strategies for managing mimetic rivalry. By vilifying an "out" group or individual, societies can channel the potential violence within the society outward against an external enemy and thus provide social cohesion. Of course, this mechanism works only if people are convinced of the rightness of their actions and unconscious of the underlying motives.

From this perspective, sports can be viewed as an important cultural arena for the expression of mimetic desire, rivalrous conflict, and scapegoating. In their more primitive manifestations, sports are imbued with violent undertones in which potential rivalries *within* a team or a community of fans are masked by the vilification of the opponent. It goes without saying that at times these conflicts are played out with frightening intensity when actual violence occurs on the field or among fans. At the same time, ideals such as "sportsmanship" provide for a more highly developed version of athletic competition in which scapegoating of opponents is expressly discouraged and the opponent is viewed as a fellow human subject. In this mode, sports can serve as an outlet for the *performance* of mimetic rivalry safely within the domain of "play."

Ironically, sports seem to occupy the role of a scapegoat in contemporary American society. Much of the current negative attention devoted to the topics of cheating, exploitation, and overinvestment in sports can be viewed as a displacement or externalization, at the cultural level, of conflicted feelings about the ubiquity of cheating, exploitation, and narcissistic overinvestments in everyday life. In this sense, the current finger pointing at sports resembles an hysterical cultural symptom, serving the important social purpose of allowing us to continue denying our complicity in unpalatable intrapsychic and interpersonal entanglements unrelated to sports.

The phenomenon of sports fan-dom is so complex that no single explanatory perspective can possibly encompass it. I suggest, however, that several psychoanalytic theories have a great deal to offer here. Sports fan-dom, of course, can be linked to the more general phenomenon of celebrity worship (Ehrlich, 2010). Kohut's (1977) self psychology has opened up understanding of the ways in which

Others, including athletes we admire and root for, can serve as self objects, helping us regulate our self-esteem through our identification with their idealized status. The inevitable problem with these self object relationships is that we find ourselves dependent on Others whom we cannot control, Others who eventually disappoint us. Thus the self-object relationship is always deeply ambivalent, and this ambivalence can be seen clearly in sports fans, even (or especially) those who seem only to admire their favorite athletes.

Large-group processes based on these dynamics are commonplace. For example, David Beckham's relationship with soccer fans in Los Angeles, after he signed a highly publicized deal to come to the U.S., illustrates this ambivalence clearly. At first, L.A. Galaxy fans were ecstatic about Beckham and showered him with love and excitement, even though he was injured during much of his first year. However, as soon as Beckham began to voice a desire to return to Europe (with some implied devaluation of the quality of U.S. soccer), fans turned on him with intense venom. Even though he was contributing to the team, he was now failing to perform the self object function for Galaxy fans of making them feel first rate instead of second rate. Most recently, Beckham has conveyed a renewed respect for American soccer, the team has been more successful, and the fans' hatred has shifted back to love.

Of course, this ambivalence also has to do with the fact that we envy those whom we admire, creating complex dynamics well described by Melanie Klein (1975) and her followers. Much as with artists and celebrities, the relationship between sports fans and athletes involves a complex symbiosis in which the athlete/celebrity/artist acts out the fantasies of the fan in exchange for the rewards (wealth, fame, special privileges, etc.) that accrue to successful public figures. There is a seamy side to this symbiotic arrangement that is mutually ignored, yet highly influential. I am referring to the physical and psychological price paid by athletes and other celebrities for lending themselves to be "used" by the public. We tend to defend against recognizing this price by focusing instead on the seemingly great advantages of famous athletes, who seem to have everything they desire and whom we envy for that reason. Lurking in the background, however, is the damage done to these individuals in the course of offering themselves to the public. The damage may be physical, like the dementia in retired football players that even the players' union refused to acknowledge until recently, or it may be primarily psychic, as with an entertainer like Michael Jackson. But it is present, and it leads to my final topic—unconscious guilt in the relationship between the fan and the athlete, a larger social version of the unconscious guilt of the parent who "seduces" the child to take the parent's desire as his own.

It is natural to assume that professional athletes are paid so well because of market forces and that this pay keeps increasing because markets have grown so impressively in recent decades. But, in a certain sense, this assumption avoids a more crucial question: why does the market value professional athletes so highly and why is their compensation so disconnected from the amount of time and effort that they are required to put forth? Might it be that there is an element of unconscious social guilt involved in the pampering of professional athletes and other performers? Might this pampering relate to our unacknowledged suspicions that, while the best years of an athlete's life might look very good indeed, the quality of that life may not be good for very long? "We," the collective sports fan, demand that professional athletes give up almost everything else in order to perform for us; and, when they cannot perform any longer or when they disappoint us, we publicly denigrate or discard them. Throughout, we maintain (and the athletes collude in this) an idealized fiction that the pact between us and them benefits them much more than it does us.

Might that dynamic partially account for the excessive mourning and idealization that occur when celebrities die? Michael Jackson, for example, was hard to idealize as a person, yet idealize him many did after his death. Might the public reaction have been caused by our feeling, unconsciously, responsible for the damage done to him by his "agreement" to serve our needs? In some small sense, are we, as fans, partnering with Michael Jackson's father?

To reiterate my main point, sports are a topic *par excellence* for applied psychoanalysis. Sports are so compelling, ubiquitous, and persistent because they touch directly on many basic needs—sexual, aggressive, and narcissistic, among others—while providing the necessary psychic safety through the mechanisms of play and the endless opportunities for disguise of conflicted needs and motives.

I have touched also on a second point, related to the first: that sports occupy a "scapegoated" position in contemporary American society. We look at exploitation and cheating in sport and denounce it righteously. But, as valid as these concerns may be, they also serve to maintain our denial that exploitation and cheating (and other sordid conduct) are part of the fabric of our everyday lives, not something confined to sports—not by a long shot. In this area, too, a psychoanalytic perspective helps to illuminate some of the obscurity surrounding sports. Indeed, far from representing separate, unrelated domains, psychoanalysis and sports, I argue, are virtually inseparable.

Note

1 Tommy John surgery is a complex procedure in which the ulnar collateral ligament (UCL) in the elbow is reconstructed using a tendon taken from elsewhere in the patient's body.

References

Butler, J. (1990), *Gender Trouble*. New York: Routledge.
Craib, I. (1994), *The Importance of Disappointment*. London: Routledge.
Diamond, M. (2008), Masculinity and its discontents: Making room for the "mother" inside the male—An essential achievement for healthy male gender identity. In: *Heterosexual Masculinities*, ed. B. Reis & R. Grossmark. New York: Analytic Press, pp. 23–54.
Drape, J. (2009a), Kansas town's values and football streak endure. *New York Times*, September 11.
Drape, J. (2009b), *Our Boys: A Perfect Season on the Plains with the Smith Center Redman*. New York: Times Books.
Ehrlich, J. (2010), Passion, rage and disbelief: Understanding the mind of the sports fan. Paper presented at the Michigan Psychoanalytic Society, Farmington Hills, MI, February 6.
Ferenczi, S. (1933), The confusion of tongues between adults and the child. In: *Final Contributions to the Problems of Psycho-Analysis*, ed. M. Balint (trans. E. Mosbacher). London: Karnac Books, 1980, pp. 156–167.
Freud, S. (1933), New introductory lectures on psycho-analysis. *Standard Edition*, 22:1–182. London: Hogarth Press, 1964.
Girard, R. (1979), *Violence and the Sacred*. Baltimore, MD: Johns Hopkins University Press.
Greenberg, J. (2001), The ambiguity of seduction in the development of Freud's thinking. *Contemporary Psychoanalysis*, 37:417–426.
Harris, A. (2009), "Fathers" and "daughters". In: *Heterosexual Masculinities*, ed. B. Reis & R. Grossmark. New York: Analytic Press, pp. 189–230.

Hirsch, I. (1999), Men's love for men: Contrasting classical American film with the *Crying Game*. *Journal of the American Academy of Psychoanalysis*, 27:151–166.

Hornby, N. (1998), *Fever Pitch*. New York: Riverhead Books.

Hyman, M. (2009), *Until It Hurts: America's Obsession with Youth Sports and How It Harms Our Kids*. Boston, MA: Beacon Press.

Klein, M. (1975), *Love, Guilt and Reparation and Other Works 1921–1945 (The Writings of Melanie Klein, Vol.1)*. New York: Free Press.

Kohut, H. (1977), *The Restoration of the Self*. New York: International Universities Press.

Lacan, J. (1949), The mirror-stage as formative of the I as revealed in psycho-analytic experience. In: *Écrits: A Selection*, (trans. A. Sheridan). New York: Norton, 1977.

Laplanche, J. (1989), *New Foundations for Psychoanalysis*. Cambridge, MA: Basil Blackwell.

Smiley, J. (1990), *Ordinary Love and Good Will*. New York: Ballantine Books.

Szymanski, S. (2009), *Playbooks and Checkbooks: An Introduction to the Economics of Modern Sports*. Princeton, NJ: Princeton University Press.

Tanenhaus, S. (2009), Andre Agassi's hate of the game. *New York Times Book Review*, November 22.

Sports and psychoanalytic therapy

Chapter 9

Early adolescence and the search for idealization through basketball and its celebrities

A developmental perspective

Christopher Bonovitz, Psy.D.

Beginning around the age of 12, I began playing tennis competitively. At the time, two of the top players in the professional tennis world were Bjorn Borg, a Swedish player with beautiful baseline ground strokes that looked effortless and a serene disposition, and John McEnroe, a temperamental American serve-and-volleyer with a dramatic flair. As rivals who faced off with each other across the major tournaments, they could not be more different. McEnroe was fiery with a "bad boy" persona, while Borg never lost his cool and, in contrast, was self-contained, steady, and regal.

As a 12-year-old boy, I was spending more time away from my family playing competitive tennis, beginning to see some of the flaws in my parents, and embracing the sport as a predominant part of my identity. I greatly admired both Borg and McEnroe for different reasons, with merged aspects from each player forming a kind of idealized object which contained some of the qualities that I wished I could possess myself – McEnroe's serve, his unique playing style, his New York City "cool," as well as Borg's top spin shots and model/movie star appearance with his long, flowing hair and headband. In various ways, I tried to adopt their behaviors and mannerisms, as together they formed an image of a role-model player that approached perfection. If I could be like them, I would fulfill a grandiose image of myself that could transform me. The image of these two players and their associated qualities that I carried around with me was a valuable resource; the attachment to them in fantasy buoyed my self-esteem when it took hits from disappointing losses and yet also inflated my grandiosity when I won a late-round match or played beyond my expectations. Borg and McEnroe were vital to the shifting of my idealization to objects who were not my parents, idealized objects that propelled me further into the world away from my family and into the realm of tennis.

This chapter draws on Kohut's (1978) discovery of idealization as a developmental need in furthering our understanding of the young adolescent's (11–13 years) search for idealization and idealized objects through basketball stars, admired figures who allow for further separation from their parental figures and bolster a sense of identity in the social world that is not directly tied to the familial environment. Young adolescence is a time of great upheaval, with rapid physical changes in the body, struggles with bigness and smallness, and a loss of protection in the world as the child grows older. Idealized sports figures for some kids become a place of refuge, where the game and the figure who thrives within it become a source of fortitude, exaltation, glory, beauty, and sensual/erotic fantasy – a forceful counter to the awkwardness and dizzying changes that can leave the young teenager feel adrift, unmoored, and fundamentally "awkward."

In this chapter I will revisit Kohut's concept of idealization as well as related concepts such as the ego ideal, briefly survey young adolescence as a developmental phase as it relates to idealization, and then apply these ideas to the search for idealization through play therapy and, more specifically, basketball with this age group of children.

Idealization as a developmental need and the traumatic loss of the object

Kohut regarded healthy narcissism as an essential component of the developmental process, balanced self-esteem in the face of disappointment and a sense of creativity and exuberance that infuses life with meaning. Healthy narcissism for Kohut grew from sufficient mirroring and idealization in relation to parental self-objects "who respond to and confirm the child's innate sense of vigor, greatness, and perfection" (Kohut, 1978–1991, Vol. 4, p. 361). Over the course of childhood, optimal development allows for self-objects to be gradually internalized that then become part of the internal structure of the self.

For my purposes here, I am concerned with idealization and the necessary experience the child requires, psychically and emotionally investing in the infallible parental figure, a self-object the child imagines as omnipotent. Idealization involves merging with the powerful image of the parental self-object, and gradually over time recognizing the flaws of his parents as he experiences ordinary disappointments and the revelation of their shortcomings (Kohut and Wolf, 1978). Optimal frustration stems from the child's survival of the gradual disillusionment with the idealized self-object, a process that allows for the internalization of this self-object's functional features (which Kohut termed transmuting internalization) and the development of ideals and values that stem from this idealized (and then de-idealized) self-object as part of the fabric of the self.

Problems enter the developmental picture with the traumatic loss of the idealized "parent imago," including traumatic disappointments that then disturb the narcissistic equilibrium and may result in what Kohut refers to as "narcissistic pathology." Traumatic loss may stem from a parent's failure in ongoing empathy, abandonment, neglect, or more generally the premature withdrawal of allowing one's self to be idealized. This kind of failure on the part of the self-object may result in the child becoming unconsciously fixated on a kind of fantasy-parent, one endowed with grandiose features and perfection that have no grounding in reality (Kohut, 1971).

Unable to experience ongoing idealization and then the gradual disappointment in the idealized self-object, the child and then later adult experiences an "intense form of hunger" from external leaders for approval and soothing that the psychic structure cannot provide on its own (Strozier, 2001). The child is vulnerable to searching out an archaic version of the early self-object, someone whom the child idealizes to temporarily fill an internal void and relies on for a sense of direction and guidance by virtue of lacking his own internal compass due to a "defect in the psychological structure." In this sort of relational configuration, one feels empty and powerless when separated from the omnipotent other. According to Kohut, only by being involved with an idealized parental self-object (such as with the analyst in an idealizing self-object transference) and then enduring the gradual disillusionment with this same object can the child internalize the self-object, and thereby himself provide the functions that the idealized object had previously fulfilled.

Early adolescence and the role of idealization in development

Ted Jacobs (1990) refers to early adolescence as the "no age time," a time where nothing is solid, a time of bodily rearrangement, making sense of a newfound "bigness," pimples, physical awkwardness, frightening and anxious feelings about the changing present and the unknown future, and rapid mood changes for seemingly no apparent reason that make regulating arousal difficult to sustain. And what's so difficult at this stage is that the child has very few explanatory frameworks to make sense of the transient upheaval, what Brady (2016) refers to as the "heaviest burden of the unexpressed." Cause and effect become very confusing as the child encounters new and uncomfortable types of sensations such as sexual urges, crushes, and acute sensitivity to others. With shifting boundaries, the adolescent is unsure of where she stands in time and space, as there is a feeling of dislocation, neither here nor there, betwixt and between (Tyson, 1996; Jacobs, 1990; Bonovitz, 2011).

There is a sense of loss among kids in this age range of 11–13, a loss of protection from the outside world that at this age cannot be fully identified. The past is still very much active in the present and beckoning the child to return to a younger state, while the future may appear daunting. There is the threat of being "young" again and returning to the mother of childhood, and yet older adolescence appears "old" and intimidating, engendering anxiety around getting older and entering a world for which the younger adolescent feels unprepared. In conjunction with this emotional experience is the onset of puberty that may result in an experience of the body as being separate from the self, existing in isolation, and containing physical shifts that feel alien and unable to symbolize as the body is ahead of the mind. As Brady (2016) describes, it is as though the adolescent is "caught in a body that is transforming and with a will of its own" (p. 14) (see Levy-Warren, 1996).

In my experience with early adolescence, especially with boys in the age range 11–13 years, there is a shift from the idealization of a parent to someone in the outside world, often a fantasied relationship with a hero of sorts. This shift may take place as the adolescent begins to see flaws in the parent, or while still in the throes of idealization of the parent. Often these objects have some sort of public status, either a famous You-Tuber, a wealthy, powerful mogul in the limelight, a musician, celebrity or athlete (in line with the theme of this chapter, I will focus on athletes). This shift in idealization from the family to a person on the outside is significant in that it is sometimes the first "love relationship" the child develops with a fantasied object other than a family or extended family member. The adolescent may come to deeply admire the person and all the qualities that are bestowed upon him or her, qualities the adolescent aspires to possess. It is often a fantasied relationship where perfection, omnipotence, and something magical are associated with the idealized object. The adolescent feels a sense of power and invincibility, an inflated sense of himself through the attachment to this object and its residency in the adolescent's mental space. It is a type of idealization in which the adolescent comes to better know his own values, beliefs, and orientation to the world through who he imagines this object to be.

An important aspect of this idealized yet imaginary relationship that pertains to the developmental process of early adolescence are those moments when the adolescent experiences the ecstasy and narcissistic completeness through some action (singing, air guitar, feigning an acrobatic dunk, etc.) associated with the idealized person. For example, Corbett (1996), in explicating "fantastic phallicism," describes driving with his nephew Alex while listening to Eminem. At one point, Alex shouts, "Uncle Kenny turn it up, turn it up!" Corbett complies, and with the "wind, the heat, and the beat" and the "cocky syncopation" they pull into the parking space as Eminem proclaims that the world belongs to us. Alex stands up on the seat, raising one fist in the air and grabbing his crotch with his other hand. Doing his best Eminem imitation, he shouts, "This is the life!"

As Corbett goes on to explain, the relational bond between he and Alex, between Alex and Eminem and his music – "imaginary big subjects" – create a kind of pulsating arousal in that moment full of aggression, assertion, omnipotence, and an "erotic muscular expansion."

In a similar vein, a cluster of the young adolescent boys that I have treated in recent years tend to adopt a superhero in the form of a National Basketball Association (NBA) player, usually an All-Star who is not only a phenomenal athlete who can seemingly defy the limits of gravity, but these days is also an entertainment celebrity with millions of followers on Instagram and appearing to live the so-called "life" – money, beauty, fame, passion, and superior athleticism. In addition to watching games, online highlight reels, and following the player on social media, there is also the adolescent's constructed image of this athlete with his familial history and social contexts and experiences shaping the dimensions of this image.

With their bodies in the throes of tumultuous change (internal and in their appearance), part of what the adolescent becomes enamored with in the NBA player is the athlete's remarkable physicality – a body that approaches near perfection in the way that it can soar through the air, perform windmill dunks, three pointers from close to the half court line, and leap to catch a ball in the air and then softly drop it in the basket all in one fell swoop. Sculpted muscles like a Greek God, tattoos, the latest flashy sneakers, and an unparalleled wardrobe full of style and eye-catching designs: what more could one ask for in an idealized object? The NBA player's body, including the sensual and erotic edges of it, fuel the arousal, aggression, and the assertion that Corbett (1996) describes "fantastic phallicism". And to maintain this sort of imaginary relationship with the NBA star the adolescent overlooks any flaws or unflattering anecdotes that pan across social media, as that kind of "news alert" has the potential to taint what exists as a powerful, narcissistic completeness.

Case of Tim: imitation, aspiration and embodiment

A pattern to my interactions with Tim, a 12-year-old boy with divorced parents, settled in over the first few months of our once, and sometimes twice a week, psychotherapy. Tim typically showed up in his school-branded gym shorts and shirt that he had just worn to athletic practice, dark knee-high dress socks, and a pair of loafers (pieces of his school dress code) – a mix of formal and playful, restrained and expressive, that represented the various contexts and activities that were a part of his orbit. Usually somewhat tired and monotone at the outset, he sat down in a chair across from mine at a table surrounded by shelves layered with games, toys, and an array of balls designed for indoor play. Sometimes accompanied with the latest iPhone, he occasionally scrolled through it as if to self-regulate and titrate our exchanges as we spoke. A verbal refrain of his was, "I don't know," laced with fatigue and confusion, unable to gather together his thoughts and feelings; it required too much effort for him, an effort that could feel futile in that moment. His re-entry from one session to the next reminded me of Beebe's analysis of mother-baby interactions in which the mother pursues the baby in the low arousal state who is preoccupied with self-regulation (Beebe and Lachmann, 2002). As the baby avoids and withdraws from the mother in a dampened-down state, the mother becomes more pursuant and at times intrusive.

With the beginning of our sessions somewhat of a slog, Tim gradually perked up if he observed something of interest in his surroundings, or if a random thought caught his attention. The change could be marked, from a dampened state to spontaneous speech, a sarcastic quip, or curiosity about technology or sports. The first type of play that Tim came up with was his own version of a Nerf-basketball game. With the hoop attached to my office's doorframe, the highlight of playing was of course imitating an array of dunks in his "air loafers" from a few of his favorite players – a windmill dunk, a flying two hander while spinning in the air, and a tomahawk dunk were all in his repertoire. Watching Tim, I had the sense that he had a visual image of these players in his mind, a highlight reel of their acrobatic plays that he carried around with him, highlights that he not only aspired to perform himself, but his adoration for their athleticism also inflated his own grandiosity as he pretended (in this fantasy play space with me) to fly across the room towards the basket in my small office that became a makeshift basketball court.

The game would usually start with us taking practice shots while deciding which players from the NBA we wanted on our self-selected team, something equivalent to an All-Star game. As Tim spun around the room with the ball, alternating between shooting, passing it to me, and bouncing the ball off the wall, he enthusiastically recounted some of the statistics stored in his extensive memory bank for each of the players bandied about – their point average, highest scoring game, number of assists per game, along with his version of the current rookies who just made the leap from college to the NBA. Throughout the warm-up and selection process, Tim was remarkably talented at impersonating his favorite players. He could mimic the distinctive style to their jump shot, their manner of dribbling, or their footwork. Interestingly, his impersonations were not just organized around the big-name stars and their signature dunks, but also the subtle, quirky mannerisms of the lesser known players. It was clear through his impersonations that Tim could visually process and map the body language of those who intrigued him. So while he could appear aloof, it was apparent that he was absorbing a lot more than he may have been letting on.

Tim's impersonations were a kind of embodiment of the player's physicality that allowed him to probe certain qualities that his heroes possessed while also selecting out traits that reflected aspects of his own personality, or ones that he aspired to adopt himself. For instance, there was Kawhi Leonard, an emerging, yet lesser known star at the time (though he would go on to become an All Star) who rarely changed his facial expression that was always serious, focused, and business-like. Leonard did not show much emotion at all – not pumping his fist when he made an important basket nor showing any frustration if a foul were called against him. Tim saw in Leonard a composure that he strove to adopt himself. Like Leonard, Tim was difficult to read, which sometimes led others to not look into his complex inner life. He did not reveal much in his facial expressions, yet he still was very much engaged and directed himself to the task at hand. He strove to play like Leonard on the court, but also looked up to his way of being in the world, not allowing distractions to derail him from his goals and ambitions.

Conflict and negotiating fouls

In the make-shift basketball game in our sessions, Tim introduced the dimension of fouls, a process of determining whether in fact the player's shot had been interfered with enough to justify a penalty, and if so granting the fouled player two free throws from the foul line. There were several aspects to this that stood out and which seemed to have relevance to Tim's current life circumstances that he was not yet able to verbalize. First, there was the job of the referee (a role usually assigned to me) to determine if the foul was indeed a foul, a process which sometimes required a replay to more closely examine the exchange. (Of course, a replay for our purposes entailed both of us re-enacting the play such that it closely approximated what took place while trying to keep our biases in check.) And, second, there was the debate as to whether the foul was a flagrant foul, and if deemed flagrant, the fouled player would receive three foul shots instead of two. In this case, it was a matter of jointly determining whether the foul was severe enough to warrant being a flagrant foul.

Though I did not make explicit links to Tim's parents' separation and the battle through their lawyers that was ongoing, my mind traveled back and forth between the game and his family's turmoil. And in contrast to the unspoken nature of what was unfolding in Tim's family, nothing was left unspoken in our game as fouls were called out and negotiated. In the connection between our game and his family, I also thought about who was responsible for these fouls, how severe were they, what were the consequences of them. Was I, now the newly appointed referee, expected to determine who was at fault, or did Tim put himself in that role? And how was aggression expressed, how flagrant or subtle was it? These were the kinds of questions I entertained as Tim and I played through our game, thoughts that of course influenced how I played and my assigned role in the game.

Conflict with winning and losing

Despite the addition of flagrant fouls and the emergence of aggression in our constructed game of basketball, the ending of our games unfolded as something that appeared to carry significance as Tim would often let me win in the final minute as the "game clock" wound down. It usually went something like this: Tim is ahead by two points with ten seconds left. Playing the part of LeBron James, he dribbles and purposefully drops the ball out of his hands so it lands right into mine. Feigning as though he trips, Tim gives me a wide-open lane to score and tie the game. Then with two seconds left, the sequence repeats itself with Tim basically handing the ball over and giving me the opportunity to score the winning basket. If I make it I win the game. If not, it is a tie. Over the course of many games, the outcome alternated with either a tie game or me winning by a basket. If I observed something to the effect that he handed me the game at the end or commented on his conflict with winning and what he might lose if he won, Tim usually gave me a look as though we both knew what was going on, and should just agree for the time being to not question our roles too much.

Tim repeatedly created a situation where he not only wanted to avoid winning the game, but also chose to leave it to me whether to defeat him or tie the game. Tim did not want the responsibility for determining the outcome. Was Tim here expressing the need to have me in control of the situation, to stay in charge and decide our fate? Was defeating me equated with carrying too much of a burden, and perhaps the guilt that came with surpassing the rival paternal figure? Did Tim already bear too much of the responsibility in his family, and so here he wanted me as the adult to be in charge of what happened? And was it an unconscious test of sorts – would I miss the shot in order to protect him from defeat, and therefore show concern for his survival and await his readiness to compete to the end? And with competition, rivalry, and winning and losing wrapped up in his parents' fighting, was he expressing the desire for a tie, an outcome where there were no winners or losers?

While there were many different ways of conceptualizing this play scenario (Oedipal dynamics, fear of success and failure, aggression as destructive, etc.), I honed in on Tim's conflict with winning in the context of the game and, in doing so, another one of his idealized objects came into play: LeBron James. Tim looked up to LeBron for his court vision, his amazing passes, his muscles, but most importantly for his ability to cohere a team together. From Tim's perspective, LeBron brought out the best in others, especially in those pressured situations when he needed others to step up their game – and his teammates usually rose to the occasion.

In dialoging with Tim about LeBron and the tension surrounding the outcome of the game, he described a wish for "no one to lose." He wished that, like LeBron, he could "bring my family together" and "make everyone get along so we are on the same team," and so one of us losing in our game was a threat to the harmony and cohesion he so longed for. Winning and losing for Tim jeopardized the cohesion, which is why he felt the need to give up the ball at the end of each game. He worried about the wellbeing and fate of the loser, as well as the triumphant victor who could misuse or even abuse their power. Tim was very curious at the end of watching games on TV whether LeBron would shake hands or hug the other players. When he did do so, Tim was always reassured that both teams could survive the competition and outcome without any destructive bitterness or resentment.

Ego ideal

It is difficult to speak of idealization without also mentioning the ego ideal, a concept that is a descendant of Freud's theory. The ego ideal is the Freudian corollary to Kohut's Idealized object, marking the transition as development progresses from primary narcissism to a period where self and object images become more distinct from one another (Milrod, 1990). The child develops a relationship in fantasy with a substitute primary love object (substitute in that the original love object is the parent) that exists outside the self, someone or something that is imbued with perfection, someone who is seen as powerful, and through the child's connection with him or her the child becomes aggrandized himself – an aggrandizement that captures an element of the perfection the child felt earlier in his life (primary narcissism).

Similar to Kohut's idealization, the ego ideal captures a developmental transition and fosters the child's relationship to important others in the outside world. Aggrandizement is not pathologized, but rather viewed as a necessary experience in order to recapture a kind of perfection which is now directed towards an object outside of one's self as opposed to primary narcissism where self and object are merged together. This object, similar to Kohut's theoretical conception, is one who embodies qualities and characteristics that the child wishes to possess for his own self.

Harrison's ego ideal and negotiating conflict between practice and the game

Harrison, a tall, stocky 12-year-old boy who closely followed NBA basketball teams and their players. He was a statistics aficionado, tracking ESPN, talking heads on sports channels, box scores, player interviews, and so on. He knew every player, their stats in college through the pros, and their strengths and weaknesses. He also played competitive basketball, but as he gradually came to compete at a higher level, his coach and parents observed that he had trouble fully exerting himself in actual games, seemingly going through the motions and passing the ball as soon as it was in his hands. In games, he avoided anything that might be construed as aggressive contact, rarely asserted himself, and backed off from the scrum of players whenever he had the opportunity. No one understood the reasons for the dramatic difference in his play from practice.

In speaking with Harrison about his play in his recent basketball games, he had little to say about it and, unlike the adults who saw him play, he was unsure how much he had become more tentative and avoidant. He did not want to regard the apparent change in his play as a problem, and in fact became quite upset if we discussed it in detail. He would start to tear up, bury his head in a pillow, and shut down. Backing off from the talking and moving our conversation into the play of Nerf-basketball, I saw a kid who became a different person from the one slumped on the couch with little or nothing to say about his own observations. Unlike how his coach and parents described Harrison on the actual court during games, here he was lively and forceful, shooting fade-away jumpers from all areas of the office, dunking the ball, alley-oops, and performing impressions of other players that were spot on. The kid who had been described as tentative on the court was nowhere to be found, and while of course the conditions were markedly different between my office and an actual game, the difference nonetheless was intriguing.

As an only child with divorced parents and a father whom he rarely saw, Harrison did not have anyone to overtly compete with in his family. His mother was depressed and terribly unsure of herself, which often left Harrison feeling as though he could inadvertently hurt her feelings. Based on the few fragments of information he knew about his father, he held a private fantasy of him as a bit of a "cowboy," someone who worked on a ranch out west, a rugged outdoorsman.

As our basketball games during our sessions became more varied, Harrison came up with the idea of combining the game "Connect Four" with basketball shots. He designed this pairing in such a way that you could reverse your Connect Four move after dropping a disc (if it was a move that might cause you to lose the game or make it more likely that you might lose) by making one of two shots in the basket from the "foul line." This was an interesting game concoction, as it was forgiving and allowed us a "redo" (his term of the opportunity to reverse a Connect Four move) rather than have to live with the consequences of a move that we wished had been different. In other words, history or the past was reversible to an extent, therefore creating a more favorable outcome. As we played through this new cycle of games, I noticed that Harrison took full advantage of the "redo," almost as though he was setting it up so that his opportunities to win the game would hinge on making the basketball shots in order to reverse his Connect Four moves and then have an opportunity to make a better move with his piece.

Going through the "redo" experience with Harrison, my mind hosted thoughts about his wish to reverse the past, to perhaps bring his father back into the family fold. I also more closely considered the idea that he had once told me early on in treatment that he refused to keep track of his own statistics during his games (despite his encyclopedic knowledge of NBA stats). When I asked him why, he told me because the "game was about the team and not the individual records." While on the one hand I found this to be an admirable stance towards his own performance, I also thought of it as a defense, a convenient justification for his passive attitude on the court, and a way to avoid caring too much about his role in the game. Interestingly, he was intent on keeping close track of our statistics – the score of each game, our respective win/loss records, and how many shots we each made in our attempts to reverse our Connect Four moves.

When I asked him about the discrepancy between how he played with me and his attitude towards his performance on the court, he compared the difference to one of his favorite NBA players, Ben Simmons of the Philadelphia 76ers. He described how much he admired Simmons' team first mentality – specifically passing and court vision – and the idea that he did not seem to be concerned with his own stats in the games. But then Harrison added, "But you know what happens to Simmons in the game?"

"What?" I replied.

Harrison looked up from the Connect Four grid and said, "He never shoots a jump shot in the game even though he can make them during practice." (Ben Simmons was a well-known young player with exceptional talent whose lack of a jump shot during games could severely hold him back from fully developing as a player.)

"What happens to him in games compared to practice?" I asked.

Harrison thought about the question for a moment, and then said, "He thinks of himself as someone who cannot shoot, and so in games he believes that even though he can make shots in practice. But shots in practice don't count so it's easier."

"So what does Simmons need to do to *redo* this belief of his?" I probed.

Harrison shot the ball from across the room as he pondered the question, "He's lucky because his dad was a professional player too." (Simmons' father indeed played professional basketball in Australia.) "So his dad could teach him and help him get more confident about his shooting form." After Harrison said this, we both knowingly looked at each other. Neither of us had mentioned the absence of Harrison's own father very much, and so it was as if he had led us into a new yet uncomfortable part of the court.

I said, "I guess he's lucky to have his father who could also be his coach."

Harrison responded, "Can we go back to the *Redo* game?"

"Sure," I said.

Discussion

The game of basketball and Harrison's ego ideal in Ben Simmons became an important vehicle for beginning the process of reconciling Harrison's sluggishness during games and understanding his relationship to aggression, performance, and concern for the larger group (team). The game of *Redo* (Harrison's creative combination), as it came to be referred to between us, allowed him to grapple with the wish to recreate the past alongside of coming to grips with an acceptance of reality. As we moved through the various phases of the games, and as they unfolded including the image of Ben Simmons as a "team player" seemingly not concerned with individual statistics and the absence of jump shots during games, what became more apparent was how Harrison's struggle with assertion during games was a way to freeze the past, to hold out for a redo, and the wish to reverse time and bring about a different sort of outcome. To play more aggressively during games, to become more invested in his stats was akin to moving forward and potentially destroying the object. As long as Harrison played half-heartedly during games he could preserve the paternal object in fantasy, a rugged ranch hand who might someday travel east to see his son.

The challenge in therapy was how to bring together the wish for a redo with the impact of his father's absence in his current life. And, of course, Harrison could not have explained this to me before his combo creation, nor could I have necessarily come up with this explanation. Indeed, he recruited the game of basketball (and Connect Four) along with its heroes for us to inhabit and live out together in order to more deeply understand the link between the absence of his father and his passivity on game day.

Conclusion

The idealized object provides the opportunity for an important developmental transition, one where the young adolescent shifts the idealization from a parent or parental figure within the family to someone outside the family. What this shift allows for is the development of a fantasied relationship with an object the child wants to be like, whose omnipotence and perfection bolster his own grandiosity, and who possesses qualities that the adolescent strives to possess himself. For Tim, it was Kawhi Leonard's even temperament, calmness, and intense focus no matter what was taking place on the court that he looked up to and hoped to cultivate within his self.

For Harrison, Ben Simmons' reluctance to shoot reflected his own hesitation during games, a fantasied relationship he used as a vehicle to work out his conflict with aggression.

But what might we say is the difference between the type of idealization that takes place with a parent and an idealized relationship with someone outside the family? First, the young adolescent is experiencing physical and emotional changes that are propelling him further into the outside world and away from the parents. As this movement takes place, the adolescent's relationships with people outside the family become more important and potentially influential. Therefore, idealized objects such as the NBA players discussed in this chapter become valuable role models as the adolescent begins to situate himself in the world and is beginning to form a conception of who he wants to be, that is partially shaped by those figures he admires in the world. Parents continue to exist in the background both as idealized and gradually de-idealized figures, and this same process then takes place outside of the family throughout adolescence. Early adolescence, specifically, is often the time of idealization of one's heroes in the outside world, often drawn from the world of celebrity.

One final note that indeed could be the seed for an entire other topic is the fact that social media plays such a large role in shaping the young adolescent's relationship to these idealized objects. With something like Instagram, you now can watch your favorite celebrity's every move throughout the day – see a video of her traveling in another country, walking her dog, hanging out on a beach with friends, backstage at a concert, and so on. This kind of access provides a window into their private (now not so private) lives, and the curating that goes along with it has an effect on the adolescent's psychic relationship to these figures. This, of course, is also true of NBA players who are indeed entertainers and celebrities these days and not just professional athletes. Seeing a video of LeBron James singing about "Taco Tuesday" with his family at the dinner table, or a picture of Kawhi Leonard playing with his friend's dog – these snippets of their everyday humanness that are now part of the public domain become an acting agent on the image the adolescent constructs of them and actively influences the kind of idealized relationship they form – and interestingly, one that also distinguishes it from their parents.

References

Beebe, B. and Lachmann, F. (2002). Organizing principles of interaction from infant research and the lifespan prediction of attachment: Application to adult treatment. *J. Infant Child Adolesc. Psychother.*, 2(4):61–89.

Bonovitz, C. (2011). The experiential modes of time in adolescence. *Psychoanal. Psychol.*, 28(1):132–144.

Brady, M. T. (2016). *The Body in Adolescence: Psychic Isolation and Physical Symptoms.* New York: Routledge.

Corbett, K. (1996). *Boyhoods: Rethinking Masculinities.* New Haven, CT: Yale University Press.

Jacobs, T. (1990). The no age time: Early adolescence and its consequences. Workshop series of the American Psychoanalytic Association, Monograph 6. *Child and Adolescent Analysis: Its Significance for Clinical Work with Adults* S. Dowling, (Ed.). New York: International Universities Press, pp. 107–121.

Kohut, H. (1971). *The Analysis of the Self; A Systematic Approach to the Psychoanalytic Treatment of Narcissistic Personality Disorders.* Madison, CT: International Universities Press.

Kohut, H. (1978–1991). *The Search For The Self: Selected Writings of Heinz Kohut: Volume 4, 1978–1991*; Ed. P. H. Ornstein. Madison, CT: International Universities Press.

Kohut, H. and Wolf, E. S. (1978). The disorders of the self and their treatment: An outline. *Int. J. Psycho-Anal.*, 59:413–425.

Levy-Warren, M. (1996). *The Adolescent Journey.* Northvale, NJ: Jason Aronson Inc.

Milrod, D. (1990). The Ego Ideal. *Psychoanal. St. Child*, 45:43–60.

Strozier, C. B. (2001). *Heinz Kohut: The Making of a Psychoanalyst.* New York: Other Press.

Tyson, P. (1996). Object relations, affect management, and psychic structure formation. *Psychoanal. St. Child*, 51:172–189.

Chapter 10

The athlete's dream

Howard M. Katz, M.D.

In their formative stages, core aspects of a person's identity and sense of self are intimately intertwined with experiences of the muscular use of one's body (Katz, 2004). In athletes, dancers, and others whose vocations and avocations are highly physical, those abiding elements of identity may be central and carry much of the weight of a person's self-concept and self-esteem. They may be well integrated with other dimensions of self for some people, while for others they are more compartmentalized. The multiform ways that these aspects of identity evolve are structured in childhood and adolescence by a person's strivings for mastery in the motor sphere, as they are played out in the context of relationships to primary objects and then to important others, who may include peers, teachers, and coaches.

The formation of one's sense of self, one's identity, also can be seen as taking place partly through acts of dreaming. While the functions of dreaming are likely multiple and not yet fully characterized, it is widely thought that they include processes of assimilating experience on the basis of affective matching (Cartwright, 1986, 1991; Hartmann, 1996), consolidation or solidification of newly acquired memory (Walker & Stickgold, 2004), and problem solving or integration of current challenges into existing schemas (Greenberg et al., 1992).[1] The particular involvement of motor control systems in the brain in the neurological processes associated with dreaming (e.g., see Solms, 1995; Maquet et al., 2000) highlights the extent to which motor learning, in particular, may be enhanced in relation to REM sleep.

In light of these ideas about the functions of dream sleep, it is reasonable to expect that for athletes, who are emotionally invested in sport endeavors and frequently working on enhancing motor performance, athletic activity in dreams may portray the challenges they face. My experience working with dedicated athletes suggests that, in some instances, dreaming plays a direct role in the motor-learning process itself, a part of the process of reconfiguring motor routines. In other instances, the motor action of the dream carries more metaphoric and symbolic significance, serving as an imagistic vehicle for the portrayal of important challenges that may be affective and interpersonal at their core. As I have suggested elsewhere (Katz, 2005), for most dreamers, the portrayal of challenges in a motor-perceptual realm of action may reflect the central role that such imagery had in the genesis of core affective experiencing. Athletes, then, may present a special case or exaggeration of what is a common trend: to portray dream problems in terms of the body's action in space and time. As some of my examples suggest, the motor learning that is so important to athletes is commonly intertwined with the affective, conflictual, and interpersonal dimensions of their lives as represented in their dreams. Linkages between these domains of thinking, feeling and acting may be seen as they appear together in the dream and waking associations to it.

Case examples

Here are six examples of dreams of athletes. The first three come from friends or associates and the latter three arose in clinical encounters.

Dream example 1: Cliff

Cliff, a talented athlete who later became a strength and conditioning professional told me of his dreams when playing high school and college football:

> When we were in season, in my dreams I was running plays all night, getting down the feeling of movement in relation to the other players and to the set up of the playing field. These were the specific plays we were working on. It was like a rehearsal.

Later Cliff became a body-builder. He would go through workouts in his dreams and, on waking, have the feeling of the muscle soreness appropriate to the actions represented in the dream. Obviously those muscles had not contracted. (Muscle paralysis is a cardinal feature of REM sleep.), but the dream representation of doing the exercise is highly associated, neuronally linked, with the imagery of the actual motor action and its resulting experience of fatigue or soreness.

Dream example 2: Arnold

Arnold, an avid amateur golfer who had lost his very athletic father several years earlier, reported the following dream.

> In my dream I'm on a driving range. There are no other players. At first I'm just hitting balls with irons, enjoying the familiar feeling of the swing and the flight of balls into an early evening sky. After a while I'm hitting wedges into this green, and add in the swing change that Ted, my teacher and friend, showed me a couple days ago. Then I notice Dad is there. He's standing behind me, and we see together that adding the new move puts a deeper flight on the ball, carries it to the back of the green. This is a very vivid image of repeating the swing with this new move included and seeing the changing pattern of ball flight in the sky. Dad is quiet, just there—as I play around with this swing change.

Like Dream Example 1, this dream portrays the adjustment of a motor routine and may be a factor in the consolidation of motor learning. But in this case, the learning process is more overtly connected with its interpersonal and emotional aspects.

Arnold's associations included the idea that he was "working on [his] swing" in sleep, "actually practicing." His father had been his first teacher, and he now noted that his warm feelings toward Ted related to his feelings about his father. His father had been a strong athlete but had suffered physical disability late in life. But in this dream his father was restored to "his stronger, younger self."

Arnold felt that the dream fixed the swing adjustment in his mind. Waking, he thought that, if he went out to the practice range or golf course that day, he would have his new move "down pat." He could also reflect on how the pleasures or frustrations of his endeavors in his sport were imbued with emotional interpersonal dimensions. The dream portrayed a wishful undoing of the loss of his father's strength, and it was expressed in terms of the athletic activity they had shared. It also reflected emotional undercurrents of his relationship with Ted, elucidating what was, in effect, a transference that amplified feelings he had in relation to his teacher.

The following dreams also concern the management of loss as a more central element—in one case a loss of one's own vitality and health, in another the loss of significant others.

Dream example 3: Toni

This is the dream of Toni, a former dancer. She told it to me years after it had occurred. She reflected on how she had had a very precise recall of it when hearing, just recently, the music that had been on the alarm clock radio as she awakened from the dream:

> The music had come into the dream. It accompanied me as I walked down the aisle of the church of my childhood, walking in a ceremonial procession. I wore a long swooping robe and carried a chalice cup. Very carefully. I moved up the aisle with the deliberate lunge of a modern dancer, very much the Martha Graham kind of lunge. Each move was measured and sacred. The procession was holy. It was clear that this was a funeral procession for one of my parents.

She commented,

> That dream preceded my father's death by a couple of years, but I knew it was coming, and, in fact, there were funerals in that very church, for my father and later my mother. I felt like the control and grace I had to have in each step in the dream procession were what I needed to find in going through those funerals, giving each of them a eulogy, saying goodbye. It felt like reaching back for something physical, musical, something in my feelings about them and about the church, all at once. And I recalled this dream, almost as if I were re-living it, at both of those funerals.

In further discussion, Toni told me of dreams and images she retains of her dance life. The imagery of the spaces in which she learned to dance recur in dreams, and she associates those places with important others, especially her teachers, who are still presences in her mind. The particular movement of her funeral dream was associated with a much beloved teacher. She recalled that she had frequently dreamed, when she was learning, of dance movement she was attempting to master, and the movement drew in other important themes in her life.

Dream example 4: Alice

Alice was an older woman who had worked with me in psychoanalysis for several years. She had been an avid and successful competitive tennis player, but now she was physically hampered by illness. At a point when she was grieving this loss of physical wellness and vitality, she reported the following dream:

> I was riding down a road on a bicycle. It was a scene near the ocean, not unlike some of the places where we rode when I was a child. At first it was slow going, like lumbering uphill in too high a gear. But I started to move more easily and it was beautiful. The wind in my face. The speed.

She talked then about the fun she had had on her bicycle as a girl, riding alone or with her sisters and friends

> We rode all over—there was a feeling like being a racer. And it sometimes became "an imagining" and felt almost like being in a race car or even being a pilot. I'd race that bike, even if it was just me. ... I wish I could be that way now.

I asked, "What way is 'that way'?" "Expansive, free, adventurous," she replied, "I could feel that way in the past, but now it seems all but lost."

Alice was sad at that moment but returned to this dream in succeeding weeks. It became a portal into that freer feeling of "an imagining," and she began to entertain thoughts about how she might now act that would enable her to partake of such feeling.

While physically restricted and having to bear the sadness of that loss of mobility, she found that in her writing and painting she could express some of that same expansive feeling. She later said that the dream imagery of herself in a state of free movement was helpful in bringing renewed energy and meaning to her creative work.

The following case also concerns the management of loss along with narcissistic injury and oedipal rivalry.

Dream example 5: Gil

Gil was a lawyer who at age 40 still played competitive hockey in a recreational league. Nearly 20 years beyond his days of playing with a top-ranked college team, his skills enabled him to keep up with younger players. While our work centered on conflicts he felt in relation to friends and family and anxieties about the competitive challenges of his law practice, hockey stories regularly punctuated the analytic hours.

One day, Gil started the hour with a report of this dream:

> I was the manager of an NHL team. I got the guys together in the locker room after one of the games and told all the veteran players, the older guys, I would not be renewing their contracts.

His first thoughts about the genesis of the dream concerned a story he had just read about young players coming up in the college ranks now. But, as he started to speak, my first image was that of his father, a talented, stand-out hockey player who came out of Canadian junior leagues decades ago. His father had seemed to be destined for the elite NHL of those days, but fell short of achieving his dream.

Gil then talked about pressures at the law firm and speculated that his dream reflected an anxiety about his job. I said that made sense to me, but I also reminded him of our recent conversation about whether he might bow out of hockey now, feeling a bit old for it.

He went on to tell me about a game the previous weekend. Of playing with younger guys, he said, "I could hold my own, maybe half the game, but I had no legs at the end. I felt upset by the end of the game, even though I had scored early and helped the team to win."

Gil said, "Well I guess we don't need old Sigmund Freud here to interpret this one, but I do have to say that I don't like to let outside forces come into my inner life."

When I asked what he thought of as "outside," he cited not only the story he had read, but his own body's letting him down. "That, my older body, feels outside, too, outside my mind." I asked about his "inner life," that he didn't want to think of as vulnerable to the exigencies of experience, and wondered aloud what aspect of his inner life might he be thinking of. He wasn't so sure what he really meant, he said, but ended the hour expressing the feeling that he just should not have a sad dream like that. I suggested that both the sad feeling and the sense he should not have it were aspects of his "inner life" we could explore further.

I said nothing about my image of his father during that session, but noted later that in the next few hours stories about his father filled the air. His father had been successful in business over the years, in spite of a limited education. His father never talked much about his glory-days playing hockey, but on visits up North to Canada, Gil would hear about those days from his uncles, who were prone to pulling out the old newspaper clippings describing his father's exploits.

Gil mentioned that his father certainly could retire now, but seemed very reluctant, in spite of his mother's wishes that he do so and the fact that Gil's uncles had both recently retired. As the story unfolded, Gil came to an idea that surprised him. He thought: Why now? Why would his father think of retiring *now*? Gil realized that he had *always* seen his father as old. For as long as he could remember, it had seemed that his father felt that his best days were behind him.

Now we could come back to the dream and connect Gil's feelings about putting his hockey days behind him and a sense he had long harbored that his father was past his prime. "Like he was washed up, even as a young father," he said with sadness. Further work led to a deepening and painful awareness that Gil had held himself back as a competitor, in work and in play, with the fantasy that it might spare his father from feeling more of his own disappointment "as a hockey player, but more, as a person."

Dream example 6: Paul

When I met Paul he was 30 years old, single, and marginally employed. For every hour working in his part-time job, he spent two hours working out and doing drills with a privately hired basketball coach or playing with other men who were mostly retired from college basketball. Paul had missed out on the chance to play in college, but he still dreamed of playing professionally "someday."

Paul was plagued for years by a repetitive dream. Always, the scene was a crowded gym with him on the basketball court. The details changed slightly from time to time, but the theme was the same: He was in "the big game" but was always "totally blowing it" in one way or another. Here is an example:

> I am in a big game with bright lights, a noisy crowd and it is close between the teams toward the end of the game. The ball comes to me. I can't handle it; I drop it; I'm all thumbs. I am trying to just pick it up, and I simply cannot even grip the ball. I wake up in a sweat.

Paul never had dreams that depicted athletic grace or accomplishment. In the typical dream he is alone in the big crowd. There are no recognizable people, only a faceless audience that will admire him if he succeeds and disdain him if he fails. Over the course of his psychotherapy, I saw that these dreams would usually recur in relation to a challenge he felt he could not meet, whether it was athletic or in another domain.

Paul had come to me after seeing several other psychiatrists who had treated him for fluctuations in mood and aggressive outbursts, variously seen as manifestations of bipolar disorder or intermittent explosive disorder. Having learned that I had a special interest in working with athletes, he hoped I might help in ways they had not. He felt that his frustration as an athlete was the central element of his problems.

Paul's angry outbursts often were related to thoughts about failures as an athlete or barriers he perceived to his performing better.

He would commonly become furious with himself over some perceived failure. Then there would be an insistent drumbeat of angry thoughts about himself or about how he was being frustrated or thwarted. At times he might break something or hurt himself, for example by banging his fist into a wall. He had been treated with a number of antidepressant, mood-stabilizing, and antipsychotic medications and had been referred to an anger management program. The angry outbursts decreased, but he remained very frustrated and was increasingly dysphoric. He ruminated and talked more and more about his failed ambitions.

Physically, Paul was a very big man. But it seemed to me that he still felt like a very small boy. As a child, Paul had never known his biological father. The stepfather, who came along when Paul was two, had always seemed detached. His mother was more emotionally involved but labile and unreliable. Paul was a rather quiet child and was often either with his mother or alone, watching television or involved in solitary play. He did poorly in school, probably owing to learning disabilities that were detected only later. He didn't make friends easily.

When he was 12 years old, Paul's growth took off. Suddenly he was the biggest boy in school. Before that, he had played sports in school and had done well. But now his entry into more structured school and town basketball programs coincided with his prodigious growth spurt to begin to fuel fantasies of a future in basketball. And he got support from some of the adults around him. He recalled that coaches seemed to think that his physical attributes and talents "could take [him] a long way" in basketball. His mother, too, became excited by his prospects.

Paul's erratic school performance was not addressed with much energy. Only later, when he was in high school and poor grades were a threat to eligibility to play, did anyone focus much attention on his academic problems. To Paul, doing well in school was only a means to the end of being able to play basketball, first in college and then in the NBA. He became highly focused on that grand goal and subordinated other interests to it almost totally. His only friends were his teammates. Even with them he had trouble getting along at times, owing to his single-minded attention to his own performance.

Paul felt frustrated by high school academic struggles, but even more by difficulties in sports, "not being on my game." He often had a streak of brilliant play followed by an almost total collapse, even in the same game. His frustration and anger at himself could be as massive as his frame. The more frustrated he became, the more obsessed he was with his fantasies of athletic success and the more trouble he had on and off the court. Ultimately, he barely finished high school and began at a community college. He described his experience there as a "disaster." He could not manage the academics and played on the basketball team for a short time before he was cut because of his erratic athletic performance.

Finally, he withdrew from school and looked for work.

Paul remained fixated on his belief that he had the talent to play professional basketball, to "take it to the next level." As he continued to practice and play, sometimes obsessively, he worked sporadically and alternated living at home or with roommates he never really befriended. He dated a bit, but young women who found him to be appealing at first eventually had trouble tolerating his obsessions, moodiness, and irritability.

When I met Paul, he was aware that he was looking for help with depressed mood and controlling his outbursts of anger, but he had no insight into how limited and unrealistic were his goals for the future. Our treatment included a search for the right combination of medications to manage his symptoms and an effort to establish a psychodynamic therapeutic relationship, which he had never had before. As we began, I could sense Paul's wish to be known and accepted, along with a profound doubt that such a thing could happen. But he could not articulate such feelings. It would take time to help him see what he wished for and how it had been expressed in his relentless and ineffective pursuit of stardom. It would take even more time together to help him become aware that to really be known in such a way required work to deepen awareness of aspects of himself that had been previously disavowed or warded off through his obsessive action.

Gradually, Paul began to come to grips with the painful reality that he was never going to achieve his long-held goal. Over several years, efforts to resuscitate his grand ambition, trying to whip his body back into shape or to manage to keep up with other guys down at the gym, alternated with more realistic efforts to imagine a future of sustaining work and personal relationships. The gratifications from these latter efforts were less grand, but more real than those he imagined in his fantasy.

Considerable psychotherapeutic work was needed to address his transference desire that I be caught up in his transcendent fantasy. I imagined that this aspect of our relationship was related to his yearnings for an absent or distant father. But Paul did not tend to think that way. He could not quite see how the rigidity of his fantasy had emanated from a need to bind vulnerability and frustration and rage, arising in part from feelings of aloneness and abandonment. Gradually, a measure of insight was achieved as he began to encounter and confront those warded-off feelings. My questioning the idea that he was a person of worth only if he succeeded on the basketball court was resisted mightily at first. He felt it as an insult, a lack of confidence in him. But over time he began to experience me as an ally who believed he was worthwhile without his achieving the grandiose goal he had set for himself. As he made some more ordinary efforts to build a work life and a few friendships, he slowly began to believe that I could admire such efforts without his being a star. This change was hard won, as Paul often struggled with me against acknowledging the step-by-step process needed to accomplish something. Moreover, he had to contend with his envy of others who had achieved more than he had in more realistic pursuits. He felt the same way in relation to me, too. I had things he did not have, and he could not leapfrog his way to them with a leap to the NBA.

Over time, his anger and frustration softened and incidents of violent lashing out fell away. The fixed elements of his fantasy faded, as he could find some other successes that were rooted in an interpersonal context. Paul could start to see how his fears and his staving off of shame had sharply narrowed his focus. He became a quieter person, sad still about things that were missing, but not so hateful of himself.

At some point he let me know that he had not had a nightmare of failing horribly on the basketball court in many months. Paul was now able to turn attention to beginning to develop a realistic career and to interpersonal relationships outside his family. In both these areas he encountered anxieties, but now he was facing them and finding some success.

Discussion: athletic dimensions of dreaming

These examples illustrate athletic dimensions of dreaming that may be observed in many people, though they might be more typical and well defined among those for whom athletic activity is a continuing major interest. The observations fall into two broad groupings.

First, for active athletes, dreaming may facilitate consolidation and integration of newly learned patterns of motor activity. Aside from any symbolic representation, the processes of REM sleep and dreaming may help in the reorganization of activation patterns underlying particular motor routines. Dreaming may play a part in the contextualization of the activity and the quest for mastery. Such contextualization may include, as in the second example, connection to the motivations, emotions, and relational contexts associated with the athletic pursuit.

Second, beyond the realm of motor learning, athletic action portrayed in a dream may be an especially apt and expressive metaphoric representation of emotional and relational challenges confronting the dreamer. The special importance of motor activity in the early development of schemas of self and the close relation between neural motor control systems and neural systems mediating the dream state suggest why this may be so.

As I have argued elsewhere (Katz, 2004, 2005), child observational and neurobiological studies suggest the significant degree to which the driving force of early development is grounded in physical activity. Moving, perceiving, and remembering are unified activities, especially in early development. A baby, at the onset of life, "is impelled to direct attention outward toward events, objects, and their properties, and the layout of the environment" (Gibson, 1988, p. 17). A small child needs to create a map of the world and his or her own place in it. In the service of that need, the child is supplied with an urge to explore the world physically and to expand that exploration continuously as development proceeds. The first bases of self-feeling emerge as the child combines kinesthetic, tactile, visual, and olfactory sensations with motor activity and recognition memory in an early form of synthesizing, integrative ego functioning. Those action patterns of early childhood are intrinsic elements of the child's seeking connection, sustenance, and affective experience in relation to others (Kestenberg, 1965, 1967). In time, these physical templates can form the basis for corporeal metaphors for affectively charged experiences of self in relation to others.

In a sense, then, every young child is an athlete, expanding and refining the repertoire of motor capability in a way that is intimately intertwined with the growing sense of self in relation to the world of inanimate and living objects. I think that the continuing resonance of this early experience is the most basic underpinning of the widespread continued interest in athletic quests throughout life. Such interest is manifested both as we run, jump, throw, catch, and dance, and as we admire accomplished dancers and heroes of elite and professional sports. It is also the seed from which grows an unfolding element of identity as "an athlete" that many young people develop in childhood and adolescence. For some people, that identity element remains central all the way through life.

Dreaming and REM sleep appear to play an important part in this building up of schemas of the self in relation to the environment. There is a growing body of evidence indicating that dreaming plays a major role in the progressive organization of memory and affect states. Empirical studies of REM sleep and dreaming in relation to memory, problem solving, and meeting affective challenges suggest a role for the dream state in revision of neural networks as guided by the affect state of the dreamer (Wilson, 2002; Walker & Stickgold, 2006). Hartmann (1996), a leading proponent of this view, underscores the way in which nonlinear processes of linking affectively significant experiences of past and present take place through dreaming, in terms of "explanatory metaphor," largely in the form of visual/spatial imagery *in motion*.

Neurobiologist Jaak Panksepp (1998) considers perceptual-motor processing of information and action as being central to the development of self sense: "I would suggest that the self-referential coherence provided by ancient and stable motor coordinates may be the very foundation for the unity of all higher forms of consciousness" (p. 309).

Panksepp has been a major investigator of the neural substrates of play. The brain systems organizing mammalian physical play, which Panksepp calls "ludic" systems, have powerful interconnections with centers mediating affect states and motor control, and overlap significantly with those activated in REM sleep: "In fact, play may be the waking functional counterpart of dreaming" (p. 295). This suggestion that patterns of activation associated with dreaming overlap significantly with those associated with waking motor play is highly speculative. But it adds an intriguing neurobiological perspective to considerations of how an athletic dimension of dreaming may play a role in shaping and reshaping not only motor routines but also, through metaphorical representation, broader schemas of oneself.

Modell (2003) has made a persuasive argument regarding the importance of body metaphor in the experience and representation of affect-laden relational patterns and self-constructs. If dreams are often concerned with recontextualizing emotionally salient problems, linking current experience with associational networks connecting to past experience, it makes sense that perceptual-motor realms of action that may have been prominent in the structuring of schemas of self in relation to the environment early in life are important modes of representation in dreams.

The imaginative function involved in creating the imagery of nocturnal dreaming contributes to an integration of learned experience with motivating affect states, revision of schemas of the self in relation to the environment, and preparation to solve problems or meet challenges in the future. These modes of mentation involve associational patterns that are more fluid and nondiscursive than most modes of waking thought. Such patterns of thought are characteristic of the implicit memory-based dimensions of experience and are dominant modes in both athletic activity and the dream state.

REM sleep dreams may be especially well suited to play a part in integration of learned motor routines and preparation for future challenges in the motor realm, as suggested by the first two dreams I presented. The athlete really may have a "dry run" of motor routines in sleep, given that in REM sleep the peripheral expression through muscle contraction is blocked. In the second of these dreams, we see as well that the relational and emotional associations of the physical activity being developed may come into play in a special way in the dream state.

The third and fourth dreams presented, those of Toni, the former dancer, and Alice, the former tennis champion, illustrate how a person very highly attuned to expressive use of the body may find that dream imagery capturing such body action is especially evocative of affective and interpersonal challenges. In both women, long-standing images of athletic grace, freedom, and control were brought to bear on a situation of loss.

Toni dreamed of an emotional challenge, the impending loss of loved ones, with a body-based representation of a response to that challenge. Anticipating the loss of her parents and having to bear her grief at their funerals, she "choreographed" her management of grief with the dignity and control she sought. In this particular "big dream," and in others she recalled, her dreaming mind called on the feeling of graceful movement she had felt as a dancer earlier in life. In her dream, the qualities of relationship and affect state are reflected by an amalgam of visual imagery, music and movement.

Alice, now hampered by age and illness, dreamed of the freedom of movement, adventurousness, and imagination she had felt riding her bicycle as a girl. This woman, who had been physically active all her life, was feeling how limits in the realm of her physical activity contributed to and also represented her broader existential concerns. She recaptured a sense of freedom in her dream, *embodied* in imagery of movement. The imagery of the dream and thoughts she and I shared about it in the course of her psychoanalysis inspired her to write and paint more freely, to try to overcome the feelings of restriction and limitation that were so painful.

The last two cases, of Gil and Paul, discussed in somewhat greater detail, illustrate ways that a patient's dreams can contribute a graphic and powerful image of the psychological situation he or she faces, particularly in a person for whom athletics has been an important organizer of self sense. In both Gil and Paul, the interpersonal underpinnings of striving as an athlete were highlighted by the dream imagery and the psychoanalytic or psychotherapeutic work with the dreams.

Paul's problems were more pervasive, emanating from a more difficult developmental background. The challenges he faced as a person could be related both to constitutional limitations and to relational deprivation in early life that led him to a primitive and rigid set of defenses against overwhelming challenges to his narcissistic equilibrium. These were evident enough in the narrative of his life and in his relation to me, but the repetitive traumatic dream was an especially vivid portrayal of what he was up against. It was also interesting and illustrative for both of us to see how the traumatic dreams recurred in relation to challenges in other aspects of his life and to note how they faded away as his ego adaptation strengthened in the course of several years of work.

Gil had a more solid sense of himself. His challenges were on a different level than those of Paul, and some were subtler and not so clearly discernible. His dream of being in a position to disappoint a group of older men because of their waning powers led him and me toward a more nuanced understanding of how he had seen his father throughout his life and how he had managed thoughts and feelings about their relationship and his own ambitions accordingly. In the work we did initially with the dream, the transference manifestations of these conflicts were muted, but when they emerged more overtly later in the course of treatment this dream came into focus again.

The dreams of athletes offer special opportunities to heighten awareness of the interplay of strivings in the sphere of motor action with one's interpersonal and emotional challenges. In the practice of sport psychology and psychiatry, such a perspective offers opportunities for deeply meaningful and effective intervention. Beyond that application of a psychoanalytic dream perspective with athletes, we may appreciate as well how their dreams offer more easily discernible examples of a more widely experienced association of imagery of the self in motion with the emotional and motivational currents of life.

Note

1 Freud (1905) himself expressed a broader view of the formation of dreams, side-by-side with his wish-fulfillment theory. He said that the meaning of a dream could be "of as many different sorts as the processes of waking thought; that in one case it would be a fulfilled wish, in another a realized fear, or again a reflection persisting on into sleep, or an intention ... or a piece of creative thought" (p. 67). But Freud continued to defend his wish fulfillment concept and never developed his interest in a more multifactorial view of dream thought.

References

Cartwright, R. (1986), Affect and dream work from an information processing point of view. *Journal of Mind and Behavior*, 7:411–427.

Cartwright, R. (1991), Dreams that work: The relation of dream incorporation to adaptation to stressful events. *Dreaming*, 1:3–10.

Freud, S. (1905), Fragment of an analysis of a case of hysteria. *Standard Edition*, 7:7–122. London: Hogarth Press, 1953.

Gibson, E.J. (1988), Exploratory behavior in the development of perceiving, acting and acquiring of knowledge. *Annual Review of Psychology*, 39:1–41.

Greenberg, R., Katz, H., Schwartz, W. & Pearlman, C. (1992), A research based reconsideration of the psychoanalytic theory of dreaming. *Journal of the American Psychoanalytic Association*, 40:531–550.

Hartmann, E. (1996), Outline for a theory on the nature and functions of dreaming. *Dreaming*, 6(2):147–170.

Katz, H.M. (2004), Motor action, emotion, and motive. *Psychoanalytic Study of the Child*, 59:122–142. New Haven, CT:Yale University Press.

Katz, H.M. (2005), The dreamer's use of space. *Journal of the American Psychoanalytic Association*, 53:1205–1234.

Kestenberg, J.S. (1965), The role of movement patterns in development—Ii. Flow of tension and effort. *Psychoanalytic Quarterly*, 34:517–563.

Kestenberg, J.S. (1967), The role of movement patterns in development—Iii. The control of shape. *Psychoanalytic Quarterly*, 36:356–409.

Maquet, P., Laureys, S., Peigneux, P., Fuchs, S., Petiau, C., Phillips, C., Aerts, J., Del Fiore, G., Degueldre, C., Meulemans, T., Luxen, A., Franck, G., Van Der Linden, M., Smith, C. and Cleeremens, A. (2000), Experience-dependent changes in cerebral activation during human REM sleep. *Nature Neuroscience*, 3:831–836.

Modell, A. (2003), *Imagination and the Meaningful Brain*. Cambridge, MA: MIT Press.

Panksepp, J. (1998), *Affective Neuroscience. The Foundations of Human and Animal Emotions*. Oxford: Oxford University Press.

Solms, M. (1995), New findings on the neurological organization of dreaming: Implications for psychoanalysis. *Psychoanalytic Quarterly*, 64:43–67.

Walker, M.P. & Stickgold, R. (2004), Sleep-dependent learning and memory consolidation. Neuron, 44:121–133.

Walker, M.P. & Stickgold, R. (2006), Sleep, memory and plasticity. Annual Review of Psychology, 57:139–166. Palo Alto, CA: Annual Reviews.

Wilson, M.A. (2002), Hippocampal memory formation, plasticity and the role of sleep. Neurobiology of Learning and Memory, 78:565–569.

Chapter 11

Recommend aerobic activity to our patients?
One psychoanalyst's perspective

John V. O'Leary, Ph.D.

I first began to appreciate the importance of aerobic exercise when I was a high school junior. As a member of a mile relay team that clocked the mile at 3:21 when the Olympic record was 3:11, we were expected to maintain the highest standards of fitness. Nonetheless, you can imagine the groans coming from the four of us when we were told by our track coach that he wanted us to join the cross-country team in our off season. He maintained this would have large effects on building our lung capacity. It meant running three to four miles a day to prepare for the fierceness of the actual course, which was two and a half miles of seemingly endless hills, and felt achingly only "up-hill" to me.

Our resistance to the coach's suggestion was immediate. Our race, the 440 X 4 (once around a football field), seemed closer to a sprint than a distance run. We argued that the need was to work on speed, not on wind power, and conveniently we could do the latter during the regular track season. But track runners are a docile group, more academic than assertive, so we reluctantly deferred to Mr. Harrington's greater wisdom. Starting as a motley group of cross-country runners, as the season progressed we got better and better. And, as becomes competitive athletes, we could hold our own by the end of the season.

The big payoff came in the regular track season, when all four of us dropped about two seconds off our regular recorded times for the quarter mile. That is an extraordinary improvement. I realized as the starting leg of the relay team, that when I reached 300 yards, three fourths of my race finished, I had remarkable wind and could easily pass other runners who were exhausted and struggling to finish. Our team's CO_2 capacity had appreciably improved over the cross-country season. I also noticed that practices were easier for me. I vomited less and generally looked forward to being with my track buddies. I was happier with my chosen sport. I know that my enhanced well-being came partly from the joy of winning, but I believe my improved fitness played a strong role as well. I noticed that I had more energy, didn't require naps after track practice, and could better concentrate on homework at night.

While this foray into aerobic fitness was highly motivated by my passion for running I have continued high intensity sports over the years. For example, I had a stretch with long-distance bicycling that lasted 20 years. This kind of commitment has translated into a self-discipline that has served me well over the ensuing years. I would like to believe that the completion of a doctorate and obtaining my certificate in psychoanalysis (taking 27 years of schooling) had something to do with having a fierce discipline. I am convinced, however, that my 40 years of clinical practice without a single day of sickness is an added benefit of that aerobic fitness.

Aerobic exercise is achieved when you are breathing hard, working up a sweat, and your activity raises your pulse rate into a zone appropriate for one's age, disease status, and level of conditioning. Common activities that are aerobic include running, cycling, swimming, walking up hills or stairs, and sports such as basketball and soccer. It strengthens your heart and lungs and trains your cardiovascular system to manage and deliver oxygen more quickly and efficiently throughout your body. Aerobic exercise uses your large muscle groups and is rhythmic in nature. To get the full aerobic benefit, the exercise ought to go on for at least 20 minutes (Foxe, 2009).

Given the extensive research on aerobic fitness and its positive impact on mood, can we make the case that a conversation about exercise ought to be in the psychoanalyst's armamentarium? This seems especially compelling when we are treating clinical depression. Is there enough data for us to say with any certainty that there may be good and powerful reasons for analysts to recommend aerobic exercise for many of their patients? This could include a recommendation for vigorous sports such as squash or swimming. *The American Psychologist* claims less than 10 percent of psychotherapists now do so (Walsh, 2011). The percent for psychoanalysts may be even lower. Not surprisingly, the ones that do are likely to exercise themselves. The latter finding has been replicated many times over (Tullich, Fortier & Hogg, 2006). This chapter will be an argument for why analysts should be familiar with the literature on exercise and at times have a dialogue about it with select patients.

What are the tradeoffs for analytic work in incorporating such a consciousness? The Surgeon General has issued a report saying that Americans should exercise at least five times a week for at least 150 minutes. Ideally, the CDC recommends twice as much time at 300 minutes a week including an appreciable aerobic component. Less than a fourth of people (23 percent) in our country are close to even these minimal standards. Yet, many experts have said that if there were a pill that gave all the beneficial effects ascribed to a steady course of aerobic exercise we would all be taking it, whatever the price tag. Some of the more established effects are: increased longevity; less likelihood of a stroke or a heart attack; lowered blood pressure; and increased lung capacity. When combined with diet, it can reduce the threat of a host of conditions like Type 2 diabetes that spring from being overweight.

At the psychological level we know about the benefits of exercise for even highly anxious individuals (DeBoer et al., 2012). Study after study has shown dramatic improvement in mood for those who exercise regularly (Tkachuk & Martin, 1999; Carek et al., 2011; Lawlor & Hopker, 2001). Aerobic exercise has also been shown to have a beneficial effect in preserving long-term and short-term memory in addition to pushing back the age of onset for potential conditions such as Alzheimer's (Netz et al., 2005; Head et al., 2012). These latter studies are based on recent research on the hippocampus, which is important for both memory and mood. This research is conclusive: a focus on exercise not only addresses the patient's mood level and reduces the anxiety tied to stress, it also motivates the patient to do something that improves self-esteem as well as sense of personal agency. It can illuminate a patient's and analyst's defenses since shame is often anchored in how our body is perceived to be working for us or against us. It can open the door to talks about health, both the analyst's and the patient's. Exercise can have a direct bearing on the patient's attendance, work output, energy level, constitution, and body image, as well as physical appearance.

Exercise and mood

Aerobic fitness clearly has benefits for the treatment of depression. It has been researched extensively. Bender (2006) tells us that exercise's beneficial impact on mild to moderate depression is one of the most studied interventions for these disorders (approaching 2000 studies to date). Where multiple studies are combined—cross sectional, prospective, and meta-analytic—they suggest that exercise is both preventive and therapeutic (Lawlor & Hopker, 2001). Aerobic exercise is effective for both short-term interventions and long-term maintenance. There appears to be a dose–response relationship, with higher intensity workouts considered to be more valuable. The problem with really vigorous exercise is that it is harder to sustain over time. It poses real compliance problems. Competitive sports have some advantages in this regard. The social, competitive, and inspirational components of sports may allow it to be better sustained over time. Later, in this chapter, I shall offer some suggestions that will encourage greater exercise compliance.

Walsh (2011) points to possible mediating factors that contribute to these antidepressant effects that span physiological, psychological, and neural pathways. Physiological mediators include changes in serotonin metabolism, improved sleep, as well as endorphin release and consequent "runner's high." Psychological factors include enhanced self-efficacy and self-esteem, as well as the interruption of negative thoughts and rumination.

Especially intriguing are the associated neurological events:

> Exercise increases brain volume (both gray and white matter), vascularization, blood flow, and functional measures. Animal studies suggest that exercise-induced changes in the hippocampus include increased neurogenesis, synaptogenesis, neuronal preservation, intraneuronal connections, and BDNF (brain-derived neurotrophic factor, the same neurotrophic factor that antidepressants upregulate) ....
>
> (Walsh, 2011, p. 584)

Exercise's impact on older adults

These effects seem to hold for older adults. Measures of lifetime stress, exercise engagement, MRI-based volumes, and cognitive performance were obtained for samples of healthy middle-aged and older adults (Head et al., 2012). The results showed a significant negative influence of stress on hippocampal volume. However, engaging in exercise moderates the effects of lifetime stress on both hippocampal volume and memory.

It is not surprising that aerobic fitness can also confer significant cognitive benefits. According to Walsh (2011) these range from enhancing academic performance in youth; to aiding with stroke recovery; reducing age-related memory loss; and lowering the risk of both Alzheimer's and non-Alzheimer's dementia in the elderly. Exercise is a valuable therapy for Alzheimer's patients that can improve intellectual capacities, social functions, emotional states, and caregiver distress. Much of this work is backed up by meta-analytic studies (Netz et al., 2005; Heinzel et al, 2015), which provide more fine-grained details about the cognitive benefits of exercise for the elderly.

The question of analytic neutrality

One concern in bringing the topic of aerobic fitness into the consulting room is that this kind of query will diminish critical aspects of the psychoanalytic experience. Psychoanalysis has a long tradition going back to Freud of being non-directive. Rosenblatt (2012) reports that therapists who utilize a psychodynamic or psychoanalytic approach frequently hold the belief that exercise dialogue can cause confusion of the therapeutic relationship and lead to complications of transference or countertransference issues. Analysts do not want to pass judgment on the patient's life. She does not give advice. The analyst strives for neutrality. She does not take positions on what should or should not be done or how the patient should handle an important aspect of a current problem. Part of the rationale behind this posture is to create a climate where the patient can arrive at his own conclusions and thereby increase his sense of personal agency. This posture is especially compelling when it follows a thoroughgoing immersion into the patient's unconscious desires and conflicts. Also, this posture helps ensure that the analyst's personal proclivities and unconscious biases will not overtake the treatment.

However, in recent times there have been several attacks on this analytic posture of being so non-directive. A brief summary of some of these historical developments follows:

First, there is the inclusion of increasingly complex ethical codes of conduct wherein the analyst is guided by national and state guidelines as to what actions to take when the patient is suicidal, or murderous, or dangerously psychotic—or even a potential danger to minors—especially when that is evident in early encounters. One simply cannot remain neutral in life-threatening situations. Rules around HIPPA compliance require this.

Secondly, there has been a massive theoretical assault within psychoanalysis itself on the concept of neutrality. Some theoretical positions like the interpersonal and the relational have argued that neutrality is not even possible when verbal and nonverbal communications are considered and where intersubjectivity is a given. Their argument is that we are constantly giving away our opinions and proclivities whether we want to or not. As Hoffman (1983) has argued, the patient always has at least a plausible view as to how we are thinking and feeling and may even have some awareness of our pathologies.

Third, the advent of psychopharmacology in the 1950's has clearly impacted our practices in ways that may undermine a passive and more neutral posture. Patients across a broad spectrum of conditions have been helped by psychotropic medication. For example, the belief is widespread among psychanalysts that a very effective treatment for major depression is the combination of an SSRI with individual psychotherapy. The case is even stronger for the patient suffering from a bipolar condition or schizophrenia. It is highly likely that many psychoanalysts have at one time or another recommended a psychotropic medication (Serani, 2002). They may even have been rather insistent about it. In other words, they may have been highly directive.

Finally, analysts have felt the freedom to add a vast array of adjunctive techniques to their analytic practices. Some of the more common adjunctive techniques are meditation, yoga practice, EMDR, and biofeedback. It has hardly mattered to these analysts that the adjunctive techniques come with a host of philosophic and ethical premises—such as the Buddhist belief in "detachment" which may be deeply at odds with certain psychoanalytic beliefs. [A notable exception is Mark Epstein's, *Thoughts without a thinker:*

Psychotherapy from a Buddhist perspective (1995). In this book Epstein goes into great detail to examine where Buddhist meditation practice and psychoanalytic treatment complement each other and also where they diverge. More importantly, he carefully reflects on the ramifications of these practices.]

Our uniqueness as a psychological science

Freud is often celebrated for establishing a psychological basis for mental disorders. He developed a theory which could explain psychological phenomena and direct psychological treatment. Cornell (1985) argues that this is often seen as a step which abandons physical and biological science for a nonphysical, psychic world. This, in turn, promotes an "either/or" view that psychological and biological factors are contradictory or mutually exclusive. On the face of it, aerobic fitness would seem to be a better fit with the biological, and physical, the "body" side of "mind-body" equation.

Freud, however, had a more complicated view. Following Cornell,

> His conviction of continuity between the two can be traced throughout his writings, from the 1895 unpublished "Project for a Scientific Psychology" through the papers on metapsychology, to "An Outline of Psychoanalysis" (1960). For example, in his 1914 paper "On Narcissism: An Introduction" he writes: "We must recollect that all our provisional ideas in psychology will someday be based on an organic substructure. This makes it probable that special substances and special chemical processes control the operation of sexuality".
>
> (p. 78)

These kinds of remarks are bound to make many psychoanalysts uneasy. Could it be that Freud's statement might better be viewed simply as a rejection of mentalism in favor of a broader and integrative scientific view? Does this not imply an integrated approach to treatment, as well?

There are other thorny issues that attend a more focused concern regarding introducing aerobic fitness into the treatment dyad. For example, how does the analyst decide which of his patients to bring this up with? There are many patients that might not be able to tolerate any discussion of exercise. Some will experience this kind of talk as judgmental and shaming. It could endanger the treatment alliance. Also, there are those who cannot tolerate exercise because of a physical condition. Thorniest of all, the analyst renders herself exposed to questions from the patient regarding her own physical health. Many analysts will draw the line at this kind of self-disclosure. In other words, there are many caveats and cautions in taking on this kind of analytic query.

Rosenblatt (2012) also asks us to consider the more conscious resistances that the patient will inevitably bring in regarding aerobic fitness. These include not having time, having another competing interest, not having the energy, low motivation, it's too overwhelming ("I'd love to exercise if I wasn't so depressed"), having a poor diet, current physical condition, no access to a gym, or simply that they are not getting the results that they want. Some of these are easy to counter, like the belief that you need a gym with a lot of elaborate equipment to work out. Others may prove more difficult.

There are also sources of resistance that the patients may be only vaguely aware of. Bender (2006) for example, locates at least three categories into which the predominant unconscious reasons for resisting physical exercises can be sorted. (1) Fears of Identity Change: individuals possess unconscious beliefs about what becoming "an exerciser" means and those beliefs are not congruent with the individual's sense of self; thus, exercise or sport activity is avoided. (2) Repressed Traumatic Association to Exercise: individuals have unconsciously associated exercise with a traumatic occurrence and therefore avoid exercise. (3) Learned Disregard for the Body: due to various circumstances, these individuals did not internalize the beliefs that the body and self are worthy and capable of being cherished, cared for, and protected. For example, when Smith-Marek (2015) prescribed exercise for her cohort of rape survivors she found half the survivors voiced discomfort exercising in the presence of men. The thought of being looked at by men while they were in outfits that may be form fitting was enough to deter the survivors from exercising in certain locations. Several survivors explained that avoiding exercising helped them to protect themselves from unwanted attention. They noted that not exercising was coupled with weight gain, maintenance of weight gain, and wearing clothing that concealed their bodies—all of which served a protective function. Smith-Marik tells us that:

> These survivors appeared to have an impression of what attributes American society views as most attractive and wanted to alter their own physical appearance so that they were not perceived to be attractive. They recognized that although this safety tactic put their health at risk, they felt that it allowed them to better protect themselves from potential perpetrators."...
>
> (p. 36)

The majority of participants explained that the physiological intensity of aerobic exercise and the associated cardiovascular impact (e.g., elevated heart rate and difficulty with their heart rate returning to baseline post-exercise) made them feel very unsafe. Survivors also had difficulty maintaining their breathing during aerobic exercise. These physiological reactions were among the reasons why several survivors preferred low impact activities and avoided aerobic exercise entirely.

All of which is to say, despite the general helpfulness of exercise for victims of trauma (Tkachuk and Martin, 1999; Carek et al., 2011), one has to be careful in its' application across the board.

Psychoanalytic resistance

Resistance for many analysts is a defining characteristic of psychoanalysis. It refers to the observation that all patients devote considerable time and energy to activities that impede their analytic progress (Adler et al., 1998). Freud's trenchant definition of "whatever interrupts the progress of analytic work" (Freud, 1964) focused exclusively on the psychoanalytic situation. Many of the original analysts tended to locate this resistance in the rebellious willfulness of a difficult patient and technical discussion was limited to specific behaviors and attitudes that avoided or obstructed the scheduling of appointments, use of the couch, payment of fees, etc. According to Adler, Banchant, et al, this limited understanding of resistance bolstered an antagonistic view of the relationship, wherein the patient's passivity and the analyst's uncontested authority became defining elements.

One must be careful in using the label "resistance" not to replicate the worst aspects of this more authoritarian perspective. For that reason, modern-day relational and interpersonal theorists have substituted concepts like, "enactment" to capture an unconscious disjuncture between analyst and patient. The latter term reflects more of an egalitarian and collusive quality. You might say blame is more likely to be a shared quality, or co-constructed.

I would hesitate to offer the term "resistance" to many of the compelling and quite conscious reasons that analysts have provided for avoiding recommendations of aerobic activity. Pollack (2001), for example, offered several reasons as to why he believes psychotherapists are not employing exercise as part of their treatments: First, exercise promotion and maintenance, as a clinical skill, typically are not included as a part of most therapists' training. Second, this chapter, notwithstanding, there is no widely held belief among mental-health professionals that increasing and maintaining exercise plays a critical and causal role in depression reduction. Third, an activist approach to exercise may be experienced by the majority of therapists as theoretically and methodologically inconsistent with their treatment approaches. Fourth, getting patients to make health-related lifestyle changes is extraordinarily difficult and requires a sophisticated understanding of the biopsychosocial domains as well as psychological ones.

A small number of studies have actually queried psychotherapists on these matters. Wishing not to embarrass patients and client resistance were listed frequently as reasons for not even addressing exercise. Many felt an exercise recommendation should be part of a medical intervention. Astin et al. (2003) reminds us that prescriptions such as mindfulness, relaxation techniques, and biofeedback have indeed become increasingly integrated into medical practice. It does not seem so far afield to suggest that a similar concern on the part of psychoanalysts could be integrated into our practices. Clearly, we have an interest in self-care, both our own and our patients. Indeed, many analysts see self-care as part of a diagnostic workup. For other analysts, improved self-care can be a powerful sign that the treatment is on the right course.

In an early study by Burks and Keeley (1989), surveys were sent out to members of Division 29 (psychotherapy) of the APA. Two hundred and thirty-two psychotherapists were asked about the amount of time spent on exercise and nutrition. Respondents indicated that their frequency of recommending diet and exercise as part of treatment ranked low. They discussed diet and exercise less often than other lifestyle factors such as alcohol consumption, drug use, and sleeping habits. it was also found that many therapists were skeptical of whether exercise actually worked in a clinical manner to improve things. More recent surveys (Hitschfeld, 2011) indicate that many therapists report that exercise fosters a sense of failure. Some of the therapists surveyed expressed the view that exercise does not fall into the domain of psychotherapy and should instead be left to physicians, physical therapists, and occupational therapists.

But there are also many positive reasons for addressing exercise including perceived symptomatic benefits, providing a client with a sense of mastery, physical benefits, enhancing the therapeutic relationship, and providing social outlets.

Precautions

When introducing exercise Tkachuk and Martin (1999) remind us that there are certain precautions that any clinician should undertake before going down this road with a patient. For example, it would be helpful to:

1. Explore the client's exercise or sport history to determine current fitness habits and past experiences in order to identify enjoyable activities critical to program adherence.
2. Educate the client about the potential physical and mental health benefits of aerobic fitness as a commitment enhancement procedure.
3. Remind patients of how important an incremental approach to exercise can be. Start off slowly and proceed very gradually to the next step.
4. Consider options to make exercise functional, such as commuting to work by walking, jogging, or biking or including home chores.
5. Take advantage of the client's environment (e.g., parks, lakes, fitness trails, home equipment) in facilitating exercise activity. Help the client choose enjoyable activities from a broad spectrum of choices.

6. Prescribe the type, duration, frequency, and intensity of the exercise program in terms of the client's current level of conditioning. Clinicians who are not trained or experienced in exercise physiology are advised to seek the assistance of a local specialist who can supervise the ongoing prescription process.
7. Attempt to facilitate exercise within a positive social milieu.
8. Assist the client to develop behavioral self-control strategies (e.g., behavioral contracting, positive reinforcement) to improve program adherence.
9. Prepare the client for recidivism and reinitiating using relapse prevention strategies.

Identity issues and self-efficacy

At the beginning of this chapter I told my story of athlete-turned-exerciser as though it was a natural or easy transition. The sad truth is that many college athletes do not make this transition. They stop any and all exercise because it is not as satisfying as competitive sports. It seems as though competitive sports have so many extrinsic rewards attached to it as compared with exercising. Examples include: scholarships, coaches, teammates, trainers, and fans. It is not a matter of lacking any internal motivation, it is just that many athletes have come to rely on external rewards in order to feel special. Exercise provides few of these externals. There is also the significance attached to being an "athlete" versus being an "exerciser." This bears on what Reifsteck et al. (2016) calls identity theory. Within their definition, parts of the self are composed of the meanings people attach to the multiple roles they typically play. Individuals will monitor and seek out behaviors that validate and reinforce their identity perceptions. When an identity is very salient, such as in the case of being an "athlete," people are more likely to engage in related behaviors. For many, exercise can feel far removed from their self-definition. Therefore, it may be more effective to direct patients who define themselves as athletes to aerobic sports.

Perhaps, one place all psychoanalysts can agree is the increased sense of self-efficacy that those who exercise, especially those who are depressed, begin to feel. Self-efficacy is important because it promotes a person's belief in his or her own ability to execute a specific behavior. It also seems central to behavior change because it guides what behaviors people choose to engage in and how they respond to challenges in changing their behaviors. People with depressive symptoms report lower self-efficacy than non-depressed people so it is particularly helpful for them (Kangas et al., 2015).

Resistance to these kinds of interventions is likely to remain as long as analysts are uninformed about the literature, have little personal experience in sports or exercising, and continue to perceive the encouragement of exercise as a difficult, near impossible undertaking, one more suited to physicians. This is especially vexing when physicians know so little about how habits are formed—which appear to be at the crux of things. Nor should they. It is not their expertise! We need to strongly consider incorporating knowledge about exercise into our analytic training. Most likely, psychoanalysts are going to avoid treatments that have not been grounded in their graduate and post-doctoral training and that seem "outside their scope of practice." They are already accused of operating within an esoteric discipline when practicing standard psychoanalysis.

Urgency

In conclusion, we are currently in an epidemic of obesity and related issues like diabetes. Our rates of depression are high and getting higher. The time for a forthright discussion about the state of American health is now. Are there patient behaviors that we can no longer afford to be neutral about? Would we be neutral if a patient lit up a cigarette during an analytic session? Psychologists and psychoanalysts need to do their part in recognizing this health crisis. It is clear from this chapter that analysts have a needed role in this endeavor. We are experts about resistance, particularly unconscious resistance, whether it comes from the patient or ourselves. We know a great deal about "conscious" and "unconscious motivation." We alone know how transference and countertransference are likely to play out in a given scenario. And finally, we also understand that any causality, whether psychological, physical, or neurological, is likely to be multi-determined in character. Each of these attributes endows us with special gifts when it comes to something as novel and complex as addressing aerobic fitness in treatment.

References

Adler, E., Bachant, J. & Lee, J. (1998). Intrapsychic and interactive dimensions of resistance: A contemporary perspective. *Psychoanalytic Psychology.* 15: 451–479.

Astin, J., Shapiro, S., Eisenberg, D. & Forys, K. (2003). Mind—body medicine: State of the sience, implications for practice. *Journal of the American Board of Family Practice.* 16: 131–147.

Bender, D. (2006) *Why don't we exercise? Towards a psychoanalytic understanding of exercise non-adherence.* Massachusetts School of Professional Psychology. ProQuest Dissertations Publishing. 3217506.

Burks, R. & Keeley, S. (1989). Exercise and diet therapy. Psychotherapists beliefs and practices. *Professional Psychology: Research and Practice.* 20: 62–64.

Carek, P., Laibstain, S. & Carek, S. (2011). Exercise for the treatment of depression and anxiety. *International Journal of Psychiatry in Medicine.* 41: 15–28.

Cornell, D. (1985). Psychoanalytic and biological perspectives on depression: Contradictory or complimentary. *Psychoanalytic Psychology.* 2: 21–34.

DeBoer, L., Powers, M., Tschig, A., Otto, M. & Smits, A. (2012). Exploring exercise as an avenue for the treatment of anxiety disorders. *Expert Review of Neurotherapeutics.* 12: 1011–1022.

Epstein, M. (1995). *Thoughts without a thinker: Psychotherapy from a Buddhist perspective.* New York: Basic Books.

Foxe, G. (2009). Hands on a hardbody: Anorexigenic culture and analytic attitudes. *American Journal of Psychoanalysis.* 69: 363–372.

Freud, S. (1964). Analysis terminable and interminable. In: J. Strachey (Ed. and Trans.), *The standard edition of the complete psychological works of Sigmund Freud,* 23: 216–253. London: Hogarth Press.

Head, D., Singh, T. & Bugg, J. (2012). The moderating role of exercise on stress-related effects on the hippocampus and memory in later adulthood. *Neuropsychology.* 26: 133–143.

Heinzel, S., Lawrence, J., Kallies, G., Gunnar, R., Rapp, M. & Heissel, A. (2015). Using exercise to fight depression in older adults; A systematic review and meta-analysis. *GeroPsych: The Journal of Gerontopsychology and Geriatric Psychiatry.* 28: 149–162.

Hitschfeld, M. (2011). *Addressing exercise in therapy: Therapist' personal exercise habits, attitudes, knowledge, and perceived barriers to addressing exercise with clients.* University of Alberta (Canada), ProQuest Dissertation Publishing, 2011. MR90285.

Hoffman, I. (1983). The patient as interpreter of the analyst's experience. *Contemporary Psychoanalysis.* 19: 389–422.

Kangas, J., Baldwin, A., Austin, S., Rosenfeld, D., Smits, J. & Rethorst, C. (2015). Examining the moderating effect of depressive symptoms on the relation between exercise and self-efficacy during the initiation of regular exercise. *Health Psychology.* 34: 556–565.

Lawlor, D. & Hopker, S. (2001). The effectiveness of exercise as an intervention in the management of depression: Systematic review and meta-regression analysis of randomized controlled trials. *British Medical Journal.* 322: 21–34.

Netz, Y., Wu, M., Becker, B. & Tenenbaum, G. (2005). Physical activity and psychological well-being in advanced age: A meta-analysis of intervention studies. *Psychology and Aging.* 20: 272–284.

Pollack, K. (2001). Exercise in treating depression; Broadening the psychotherapist's role. *Journal of Clinical Psychology*, 57(11): 1289–1300.

Reifsteck, E., Gill, D. & Labban, J. (2016). "Athletes" and "exercisers": Understanding identity, motivation and physical activity participation in former college athletes. *Sport, Exercise, and Performance Psychology.* 5: 25–38.

Rosenblatt, A. (2012). *Factors related to psychologists' recommendation of physical exercise to depressed clients.* Adler School of Professional Psychology, ProQuest Dissertations Publishing. 3569395.

Serani, D. (2002). The analyst in the pharmacy. *Journal of Contemporary Psychotherapy.* Fall 32, 2–3: ProQuest Central pg. 229.

Smith-Marek, E. (2015). *The experience of exercise: Women survivors of sexual violence.* Kansas State University. ProQuest Dissertations Publishing. 3708491.

Tkachuk, G. A. & Martin, G. L. (1999). Exercise therapy for patients with psychiatric disorders: Research and clinical implications. *Professional Psychology; Research and Practice.* 30: 275–282.

Tullich, H., Fortier, M. & Hogg, W. (2006). Physical activity counseling in primary care; who has and who should be counseling? *Patient Education Counseling.* 64(1–3): 6–20.

Walsh, R. (2011). Lifestyle and mental health. *American Psychologist.* 66: 579–592.

Chapter 12

Marathons, mothering, and the maelstrom of trauma

Running away with yourself

Stephanie Roth-Goldberg, LCSW-R, CEDS

In 1967 Katherine Switzer became the first woman to run the Boston Marathon. Prior to that long-distance running was seen as only a man's sport. Women have now been running marathons for almost a half century even though a certain subset of women take this sport to dangerous places. This chapter will examine the dynamic quality of women's marathon running which can serve both as a vehicle for self-esteem and empowerment, yet under particular circumstances may also function as a self-harming experience marked by dissociation and disavowal. This chapter will look at the body state (J. Petrucelli, 2015) of the dissociated runner. In such dissociation the body inhabits a state that is disconnected to other aspects of the experiential self. When a person is dissociated while running the body is solely in its "running state." Within the analytic dyad, the two women in this chapter found ways to reclaim their bodies in a less dissociated manner, enabling them to experience the joy in running marathons.

I am going to examine the meaning running has for women that I have treated psychotherapeutically.[1] For many women running serves as a means of discovering power, strength, and community. However, for some in distance running, what was once power and strength can lead to the disavowal of bodily experience. An anecdote I often hear from patients is "I went for a run to change my mood" or "I couldn't stop crying so I went for a run." When there is a history of trauma, running can serve as the vehicle for dissociation. What begins as an attempt to self-regulate painful emotions can quickly become self-harming. The self-harm, which takes place when there is dissociation and disavowal of one's bodily experiences, often ends in an injury that prohibits further running and further escape. My goal is to help traumatized patients transition from a pathological attempt at self-regulation to a more adaptive one. By giving voice and experience to the full range of vulnerable, painful, and powerful self-states that running may enact or inspire, it can again become a vehicle for greater bodily attunement and psychological self-awareness.

As an analyst and an endurance athlete who can relate to the "symptom" of running, female distance runners make up a good portion of my practice. When patients are referred to me, there is often a disclosure from the referral source letting my patients know I am a runner well before they initiate contact. The doctors, physical therapists, and dietitians who make the referrals believe that these disclosures are necessary, as patients will only call once they've learned that I am a runner and an endurance athlete. For this subset of women, the knowledge that I am an athlete somehow makes the connection worth exploring. I am familiar with the language of running, the local race calendar in New York City, as well as the intense passion running can ignite.

The women I work with often find power in their strength and endurance. Many patients run to reclaim their bodies from trauma, running allows them to feel powerful, something they've seldom experienced. However, for many, this attempt to claim power can become dissociative, often causing injuries. Because so many patients know I am a runner, patients often begin therapy with the idea that I will support their continuing to run, no matter how harmful it proves to be. The work I do sometimes supports running, but often does not. This gets played out in the transference in a variety of ways. The goal of the work is often to create felt experiences and focus on feeling one's pain and treating their injuries, both psychological and physical before returning to running. For many of my patients, the goal of lacing up their sneakers, tying their hair in a ponytail, and returning to cross a finish line is achievable, but sometimes it takes a long time to get back there.

Long-distance running, put simply, is the continuous act of putting one foot in front of the other. But it isn't that simple. There is a lot of self-care to be done outside of typical training hours, including nourishing one's body with proper nutrients, stretching, and strength training. To endure the pain of long distance requires a certain level of bodily disconnect – not just from the pain itself but from the corollary desire to give up – but there is always a need to check in and distinguish between the discomfort of pushing your body long distances and the pain that comes from an injury. Being able to make the distinction and honor it – to feel what is happening inside your body and acknowledge it – is the most enjoyable, attuned way to complete a race.

Running doesn't consciously start as self-harming, but it can quickly escalate in that direction. Many of the women I see in my practice were abused and neglected in childhood. They find power in themselves in a way they didn't know they could before – by dissociating from intolerable feelings and self-states through running. The difference with running, as opposed to other harmful behaviors, such as bingeing and purging, is that there is a healthy way to participate in running. Runners can be healthy and feel powerful, without repressing feelings and disassociating from their bodies. The task then for analysis is not simply to help these patients to stop acting-out, but to help transform their running from a self-harming and dissociative activity to a vehicle of self-empowerment and a way of creating stronger connections between mind and body.

Case vignette

O was referred to me by her physical therapist after being diagnosed with osteoporosis in her early 30s. Her bones were weak and breaking frequently, but she refused to stop running. Even after she was prescribed medication that was to be injected into her stomach daily to help rebuild her bones, she continued her relentless running; often rising in the very early hours of the morning, before sunrise, after a sleepless night, to lace up her sneakers before spending a day in a job that contributed to her feelings of worthlessness and loneliness. Rather than empowering her, running had become an activity of self-harm. Like many of my female patients, O agreed to see me because I was a runner, and she believed I could understand her desire to run, even though her body had other plans. She had been told to go to therapy after previous injuries, but she was "not interested in talking." Indeed, O often begins our sessions by reminding me that she is "not interested in talking." As a result, we spend a lot of time in silence, permitting her the space to feel whatever she is feeling, rather than running from it.

O describes feeling worthless throughout most of her life, and only finding confidence and worth in her running capabilities. O grew up one of six children in an Orthodox Jewish family and recalls early on being made to feel that her only purpose was to marry and procreate. She states that as long as she can recall she was not interested in doing either. O describes herself as being a "latchkey kid" before there were latchkey kids, coming home to an empty home every day, feeling terribly alone.

O does not describe her mother as nurturing; she does not feel seen by her mother or understood. The youngest girl and the youngest child, O describes her parents as busy and preoccupied. She doesn't recall care from her mother, or her older sisters. Her father was largely absent, running his store, teaching at the local Yeshiva, and often could be found praying at temple. Her mother, also a teacher at the Yeshiva, was responsible for the six children and the home, and then a growing number of grandchildren. O's older sisters took care of her when she was very young, although, little more than children themselves, they could not fulfill a true motherly role, and thus O did not have the experience of learning her body or having an attuned mother. As a direct result, she does not have a realistic body image or a sense of being in her body.

As a late adolescent, O suffered from severe anorexia, which brought shame to her family. She began cutting herself at age of twelve in an attempt to "feel more." She ate enough to survive, while hoping to decrease her intake enough not to survive. O often expressed her desire to starve to death. Her parents were hesitant to get her treatment as they believed it would interfere with her eligibility to be married. Eventually, O did get treatment and states that as long as she looks normal, no one is concerned with her. This is a theme that arises over and over in O's adult life. O expresses because she "looks normal, or fat even" no one worries about her, no one cares whether she is miserable. She often states that because she appears normal, no one can see anything or everything that is wrong. O is not objectively fat, she is often is medically underweight.

One of the first pieces of information I learned about O was that she had an Alter-G, Anti-Gravity treadmill in her home. This is a treadmill most often found and installed in physical therapy clinics or used by professional runners. The goal of this machine is to reduce the impact on one's body. When strapped into the machine, the user is able to run while being suspended slightly above the belt of the treadmill. This machine literally allows one to run without feeling impact. The runner does not feel their feet touch the ground. O found she was using the treadmill so frequently at her physical therapist's office due to injury that she spent all of her savings to purchase this very expensive machine.

In our treatment, this treadmill would come to symbolize how stuck O felt in life. By manipulating electrical outlets and rearranging her space, she installed the treadmill in her parents' home, where she lives, where she feels bound by religious rules she does not believe in, and trapped in a job that will not afford her the ability to get an apartment big enough for her and her treadmill. She will be disowned by her family if she leaves before marriage, so she stays, and uses running as a mechanism to defy her parents, who believe running is a sport for men.

O is a fast runner. She began running and quickly realized she was good at it. However, any race that she runs without defeating a personal record, is a failure, one which she berates herself over and internally tortures herself about. O's organization of self is that of a failure, she deeply experiences that nothing she does is good enough. Without ever developing a meaningful bodily experience, she treats her body as something disconnected from her. The clearest illustration of O's disconnection can be found in her first race. O finished her first half-marathon with two pelvic fractures. She ran through the pain, through the injuries, and crossed the finish line among the top women's runners in the field.

She eats so that she can run, but when injured badly enough that running is physically impossible, she retreats to food restriction and other self-harming behaviors, including cutting, and sometimes piercings from a professional. These behaviors are done in secret, she is full of shame and feels alone when she cannot run. O will swim when she cannot run, but is limited by her parents rules that she only swim in the pool hours designated for women. Running, however, is something she does in the open and while defiant, also not isolating. O is part of a running team. When she races she does so in short sleeves, another act of defiance.

O and I have sat in silence for entire sessions, particularly when O is injured and feels as though her world has crumbled. She becomes angry and disappointed, and believes no amount of feeling or talking will offer her the same escape running offered because the only time O feels powerful in her body is when she can run or damage the body.

In the sessions during which O is injured and incapable of running, after an initial period of silence, she will show me a new piercing or, begrudgingly, discuss her cutting providing little detail. She allows me to help her represent her feelings, see her scars, and talk about them, even if on the outside she "looks normal" and has been taught to believe that looking "normal" is the equivalent to desirable and worthy. These moments mark the first time she allows herself to verbalize her feelings and her experiences of self-harm. It is through these conversations that we work together to let O be in her body, without shame and without expectation of being anything but as she is. As O has become more comfortable in our sessions and more accepting of the idea that disconnecting from your body is not actually an act of empowerment, she has begun to break her silence by admitting some part of her body is hurting and confessing that she needs to rest. Each time she is able to make these kinds of connections, we attempt to process and acknowledge the loss of her ability to run, even if temporary. Just acknowledging that something is hurting before it becomes an injury is now empowering for O. She is learning to feel pain and honor it, rather than disavow the experience thus creating an injury.

When I am with O I feel the desire to hug her, let her know she is worthy of care and comfort. If O had a good enough mother, would she allow herself to be a good enough person? For now, she has accepted that she is a good enough runner, and has come to learn that when she honors her body, she can continue to run.

No one in O's family has ever come to a race, they don't acknowledge the medals or the prizes she brings home. In 2015 when I did not run the NYC Marathon, I decided to spend that year cheering. I tracked O's time and was prepared to call her name when she passed me. I did so as she zipped past me at mile 24, she heard me and waved unexpectedly. If you are an endurance athlete in New York City, you are either running the marathon or cheering for it the first Sunday of every November.

When she came into session the following week, two days after the race, she was grateful to have heard her name being called. Having never had the experience of actually being seen during a race, hearing someone call her name was a powerful experience. She went on to finish in her best time ensuring her spot in the elite Boston Marathon. She now sends me pictures of her running watch with times after she completes races she is happy with, allowing her to have someone cheer for her from afar.

O is angry with the caution she must exercise due to her aging bones, but through silence, wherein she permits her feelings to emerge, and open discussion of her feelings and behaviors, she is able to take care of herself differently. Two years into our work together, O ran a successful marathon, she ran her fastest one-mile race, a goal she fought for without injury. It took a long time to get O to a place wherein she was capable of beginning a run only after properly nourishing her body and not running to escape from negative experiences.

Case vignette

One of N's first memories is of crying at the top of stairs, while her parents watched television downstairs. No one ever took N's hand and showed her that her room and her bed were safe, that there were no monsters lurking under the bed or in the closet.

When N was seven or eight years old she was sexually abused by her neighbor. She was awoken in the middle of the night and taken from her bed. By this time, N already recalls being a quiet, timid girl whose needs and feelings would be ignored. The abuse went on for several years. Throughout her life, N reports waking up startled in the middle of the night, sweating. Through our analysis she was able to identify that sleeping still does not feel safe. She cannot recall a time when sleeping was safe.

N is an accomplished runner, having run marathons all over the world. A difficulty she was facing in her eating disorder treatment were the rules against exercise, disabling her from participating in what she described as the one thing in life that brought her joy. After an in-depth exploration of N's running history, we quickly realized joy was not what she felt while running. There was a freedom in running N did not feel anywhere else. She felt accomplished and safe.

She felt powerful, and was using her body on her terms in ways that felt positive, thereby invoking a sense of control that she'd been missing. Still for N, running was transforming into a harmful activity. The rigid rules and strict schedule she imposed on herself prevented her from doing much else – too many early training runs – and often left her weak and injured. While running, she felt she wasn't in danger of being violated, but she'd become so dissociated from her own body that she suffered numerous injuries; completing races that often required an IV of iron and other fluids afterward. She frequently finished races with dangerously low blood pressure and relied on cortisone injections to feel less physical pain in her ankles and feet.

It became clear that the goal of our initial treatment would not be to get N back to running, but, to use the analysis to honor a state of being where N was participating in her experience and acknowledging when it was too difficult to do so.

Part of my work with N was noticing when she would mentally leave the room and become dissociated. The self-state that was present would disappear and N would become a bit quieter and more compliant. Careful attunement was required to be with N in her states of present moments and to notice her dissociative ones. N is used to people ignoring her needs, and has grown used to being physically in a room while not at all being in the room mentally.

After just a few weeks of working with N she was able to admit that her foot had been bothering her since she entered eating disorder treatment seven months prior. She was also able to express concern that the treatment center was ignoring the severity of her food restriction. She was honest with her team in outpatient about her lack of food intake. The facility kept her in outpatient while she was in need of residential treatment. The acknowledgment of N's struggle with her eating disorder and with the treatment center marked the beginning of an analytic relationship where she feels seen and heard, tended to. It did not take long for N to decide to enter inpatient treatment after bringing her concern to analysis. She has since looked back at our beginning and realized she needed the acknowledgment and support from another person to advocate for herself. While in inpatient treatment she agreed to get her foot and tendon treated by a doctor only when it was clear that she again would not be allowed to run. Feeling the pain in her foot and admitting it was there, telling someone she was in need and letting them treat her, was a breakthrough for N. For months prior, N had walked around New York City, participated in a job, which required her to be on her feet for twelve hours a day, all with a torn tendon. N had surgery to repair the tendon and subsequently spent six weeks on crutches followed by several weeks in a walker boot. She returned from residential treatment on the crutches and, after several sessions of struggling to balance on crutches and push the buzzer, eventually had to rely on me to open the door to the waiting room. She was feeling her pain and was in need of help and increasingly willing to name and accept it. Emotionally, she was feeling the pain of not running, of losing that sense of power and control, and being in her injured body. She was feeling the difficulty of inhabiting her body, letting others be with her in her emotional discomfort, and allowing herself to cry to me and express a bit of anger. We used this experience as another way to reclaim her body, the goal eventually to reclaim her running, to heal her body and to allow her mind to lead the way to a finish line. But this time, with an attunement and empowerment N was not bound to the dissociated state and injured body she'd been running in before.

N and I are in the infancy of our work together, though we have worked for nearly two years in psychoanalysis. N struggles to find her voice and is afraid to know her desires and needs. About eighteen months into the treatment, N had a scheduling request: she needed to move one of our evening sessions to accommodate a work commitment. After being aware of the need for several weeks, she came in one day, sat on the couch, and tearfully admitted she was having dreams of me kicking her out of treatment. When we explored and analyzed the dreams, she was able to acknowledge that she was so used to being neglected that the idea she needed to ask for something was terrifying. She was afraid if she was not able to come three times a week, I would fire her as a patient altogether. The concern ultimately drilled down to N's fear that if she was not a perfect patient, with perfect scheduling compliance, then she was not good enough to be a patient at all. We sat with the dreams, with the tears, allowing space for N to cry and me to acknowledge her pain, something her own mother was unable or unwilling to do, something she stopped looking to her mother for very early in life.

My pull with N is to meet every need, to change my schedule and accommodate her. I want her to know her needs are valid and she is allowed to have needs, that people who care about her will meet them. I want to reward her bravery every time she expresses an emotion and allows herself to stay mentally in the room with me and her feelings, stay in her body and feel whatever she is feeling. I want to be the good enough mother N never experienced.

I was, however, unable to meet this particular scheduling need. N's work commitment would last for a few months and I had to sit with my own anxiety around disappointing her. During those weeks, N had several more dreams about my "firing her, kicking her out, or ignoring the need to find a new time." Ignoring her need played a crucial role in our working through this. My role was to assure her that her needs were valid, that I might not be able to immediately meet the need, but we would, together, attend to her feelings, as well as her fears.

My role as an analyst was to hold the frame, maintain the boundaries, and work through this difficulty. I couldn't switch my schedule to accommodate her, although part of me wanted to. We did eventually find a time that worked for both of us and N felt contained as we struggled through the scheduling hiccup.

N is not back to running marathons; her relationship with running is different now. She runs to get some time away from electronics, the stress of her job. She runs to feel herself in her body. She runs when she wants, there is no training schedule, sometimes there are weeks between runs. She has accepted that she is a good enough runner through the good enough mothering that our analysis is providing. She sometimes feels pain in her feet and has been treated for arthritis that developed. The doctor's suspect the arthritis might be due to overuse.

Neither N nor O experienced their caregivers as comforting, and neither allowed themselves a friend or therapist to run by their side and be there with them. In the analytic dyad we are now able to work are side by side exploring the meaning of their lives, the feelings in their bodies. We are working to defend their desires and their existence. For O being cheered for along the marathon course was the mothering she needed to really open to me and become present in the experience of her body. For N, finding a time for our third session, allowing her to cry and contain those feelings are bringing her to a place of having feeling in her body and her experience. I remain hopeful that, one day if she desires, she will run another marathon.

Note

1 While this chapter focuses on women who run marathons, there is no assumption being made that these experiences do not happen to men. My clinical work has been primarily with female runners, which is what the paper is discussing.

Reference

Petrucelli, J. (2015). *Body-states*. New York, NY: Routledge, Taylor & Francis.

Index

abuse 182
addiction 5, 56–57
Adler, E. 169
adolescence 115, 127–128, 130–142, 179
Adorno, T. 46
advertising 44
aerobic exercise 161–175
affect regulation 86
affiliation 1–2, 6
Agassi, André 112
agency 15, 163, 165
aggrandizement 137
aggression 12, 18, 40–41, 60, 121; adolescence 131, 132, 136, 138, 141, 142; expression of 54, 55; fans 62; tennis 82
Alou, Felipe 68
Alpers, Paul 100
altered states 12
Althusser, L. 19
Alzheimer's patients 163, 165
analytic dyad 65, 185
Angell, Roger 21, 22, 23, 24, 25
anger 80, 81, 82, 151–152, 153
anorexia 179
anxiety 4, 54; adolescence 130; athletes' dreams 149; baseball 32; benefits of exercise 163
applied psychoanalysis 114
Ardour, Ann 13
arousal 84–85, 132
Arsenal 99, 100, 113
Ashburn, Richie 98
Astin, J. 170
athletes 38, 42–48, 51; dreams 144–160; identity 172; passion 103, 104; psychological damage to 120–121; self-object relationship 119–120; stereotyping of 60n3
Aviram, Ron 104

Bachant, J. 169
Balint, Michael 11–12, 16, 18, 19, 21, 23, 24
ballparks 64–65
Barber, Red 26, 98
Barta, Roger 112, 115, 116
Barthes, Roland 37, 41
baseball 2, 41, 62–79; aggression 55; danger 60; depth and spaciousness 64–65; fans 71, 72–74, 77n5, 96–97; gender 11–16, 18–19, 27–29, 30–32; humility 36; hyperstimulation 46–47; owners 45; passion 105–106; rituals 98; rules 66, 75–76; situations and decisions 66–70; statistics 71–72; steroids 43–44; time 20–22, 70–71, 74, 75; words 22–26
Baseball Annie 27, 29
basketball 2, 17, 41, 43, 74; adolescence 132, 133–142; aerobic exercise 162; athletes' dreams 151–154; gambling 20; hyperstimulation 46–47; owners 45; self-criticism 38–39; time 70
batters 67, 71, 98
Beckham, David 120
Beebe, B. 133
belonging 6, 7
Bender, D. 164, 168
Berg, Moe 68, 69
Bettelheim, B. 63
Bevens, Floyd 98
Billow, R. M. 106
biofeedback 170

Bion, W. R. 106, 107
bipolar conflict 70
bisexuality 12, 16
Black Sox 22, 33n4
Blumberg, Philip 1, 58
body 18, 19, 51; adolescence 130; athletes' dreams 145, 150, 158; baseball 30–31; basketball 132; female 28; idealization 115; identity linked to 144; learned disregard for the 168; runners 176–178, 179, 181, 183–184, 185–186; tennis 81, 82, 83, 84, 85
body-building 145–146
bonding 103, 104–105, 106–107
Bonds, Barry 72
Bonovitz, Chris 127–143
Borg, Bjorn 80, 89, 127–128
Boston Red Sox 21, 33n9, 69, 74, 96
Boswell, Thomas 62, 63, 77n5
boundaries 60, 88–89
boxing 60
Brady, M. T. 130
brain 73, 88, 95, 144, 156–157, 164
Brohm, J. M. 19
Brooklyn Dodgers 8n3, 96–97, 99, 100
Buddhist meditation 166–167
Bull Durham (1988) 27
Burks, R. 170–171
Butler, Judith 15, 30, 114, 116

Campanella, Roy 98
capitalism 7, 18–19, 38
Carnochan, W. B. 95–101, 103
catchers 68, 98
celebrities 119–121, 142
Chasseguet-Smirgel, J. 30
cheating 119, 122
Chester, Hilda 27, 32, 34n11
children 42, 53, 55; ego ideal 137; fandom 105–106; idealization of parental self-object 128, 142; parenting 113, 117–118, 121; physical development 155–156; play 54
Chile 19
choking 83
Cincinnati Reds 29
class 17, 18, 21, 22
Clijsters, Kim 80–81
clothing 5–6
clutching 83
coaches 55, 56, 115
codes of conduct 166
combat 41

community 6, 7
competition 7, 21, 55, 84, 136
competitiveness 55, 62, 81, 82, 84, 106
concentration 84
confidence 84
conflict 19, 37, 114–115; bipolar 70; mimetic rivalry 118–119; narcissistic 118; psychological 82
Connors, Jimmy 80, 81, 89
containment 65, 104, 106, 107, 108, 110
Cooper, Steven 36–49
Corbett, K. 39, 131, 132
Cornell, D. 167
countertransference 106, 165, 173
Craib, I. 113
cricket 16
crime 43
critical theory 16
cultural feminism 12
culture 114–115, 118–119
cycling 162, 171

dance 60, 147–148, 158
danger 60
Dean brothers 30
decisions: baseball 67–69, 71; tennis 83, 85
Dedrickson, Babe 28
defenses 158–159
defensiveness 58
degradation 37, 44, 46, 51
DeLillo, D. 64, 77n3
depression 2, 58, 62; aerobic exercise 164, 170; group psychotherapy 107–108, 109–110; increase in 173; losing 63; medication 166; ruminative 3; self-efficacy 172–173
devaluation of sports 50–51
Diamond, M. 116
diet 170–171
DiMaggio, Joe 21, 99
discourse 22–23
disloyalty 44, 45
dissociation: fans 44, 46; running 176–177, 183; tennis 83, 86, 87
distraction 5
doubles tennis 85–86
Drape, J. 112
dreams 144–160, 184, 185
drug use 43–44
Dykstra, Len 30
dynamic shifts 70
dysphoria 4, 5, 152

eating 12, 24
eating disorders 179, 182, 183
Edward, Harry 16–17
ego ideal 137, 140–141
ego identity 104
embodied simulation 73
"emotional mind" 85
emotions 53, 56–57, 62; baseball 73–74; containment 106; group psychotherapy 109; passion 103–104; running 176; tennis 80–81, 82
enactment 170
engrossment 70
envy 47
Epstein, Mark 166–167
equality 20
Eros 18
errors 85
ethical codes of conduct 166
ethnicity 18
Evert, Chris 80
Exely, Frederick 22
exploitation 119, 122

fairness 18, 20
family 105
fans 1–8, 58–59, 95–101; baseball 71, 72–74, 77n5, 96–97; clothing 6; devaluation of sports 51; dissociation 44; Hilda Chester 27, 32, 34n11; as Lacanian subjects 115; narcissistic identification 62; passion 102–106; psychoanalytic perspective 119–120; rivalry 119; "spechating" 37, 45–48; tribalism 6–7
fantastic phallicism 39, 40
fantasy: athlete's career fantasies 152–153, 154; grandiose 39, 40; heroism 42; irrational 38; nostalgia 48; transitional space 54
fantasy sports 14, 33n5
Federer, Roger 80, 88, 97–98
femininity 28, 32, 116
feminism 12, 15, 27, 29
Fever Pitch (Hornby) 99–100, 113
Field of Dreams (1989) 21–22
Florida Marlins 45
Fogerty, John 39
football 17, 32, 74; aggression 55; danger 60; gambling 20; owners 45; strike 22; time 70; *see also* soccer
Foucault, M. 16

fouls 134–135
free association 41
freedom 65–66, 76
freezing 82–83
Freud, Sigmund 23, 38, 63, 77n4; dreams 159n1; ego ideal 137; id 59; psychoanalytic relationship 66; psychological and physical bases of mental disorders 167; reason 60; resistance 169
Frontiere, Georgianne 29
fun 18, 52, 54

Gaffney, Jabar 43
gambling 5, 20
gaze 15
gender: baseball 11–16, 18–19, 27–29, 30–32; Butler 114, 116
Giamatti, Bart 30, 34n13, 74–75, 78n9
Gibson, Bob 30
Gibson, E. J. 155
Girard, René 114, 118–119
Gmelch, George 98
golf 51, 55, 56, 65, 146–147
Goodman, Cary 18, 21
Goodwin, Doris Kearns 96, 97, 98–99
Gossage, Goose 31
Gould, Stephen Jay 77n6
grandiosity 38–39, 40, 127–128, 129, 133, 141
Greenberg, J. 117
Greif, Don 50–61, 105
group psychotherapy 106–110
guilt 118, 121, 136

Halberstam, David 99
Hamill, Pete 96
Hansell, James 112–123
Harris, Adrienne 11–35, 117
Hartmann, E. 156
hate 45–47
healing 106, 108, 110
health 163, 173
Hemingway, E. 102
Henrich, Tommy 99
heroism 41, 42
heteronormativity 26, 116
"Hilda" (Dodgers fan) 27, 32, 34n11
hippocampus 163, 164, 165
Hirsch, Irwin 1–8, 58
hockey 32, 37, 41; athletes' dreams 149–151; danger 60; fans 103; time 70
Hodges, Russ 96

Index

Hoffman, I. 166
Hohler, Bob 43
Hornby, Nick 99–100, 113
hubris 36
humility 36, 39
Hyman, Mark 113, 114–115, 118
hyper-reality 75, 76
hyperstimulation 46–47

id 59
idealization 37, 38, 42, 48; adolescence 127–128, 130–132, 141–142; athletic body 115; celebrity worship 119–120, 121; parental self-object 128–130
identification 8n3, 30, 44; baseball 73; clothing 6; narcissistic 62; passion 5–6, 103, 104–105, 106–107, 110; vicarious 37, 42
identity 58, 60, 83–84; adolescence 127; athletes 156, 172; body linked to 144; fear of identity change 168; gender 116; Laplanche 117; male 32; narcissistic 116–117; passion 107; postmodern feminism 29
ideology 15, 16–20, 26, 29
imagery 157, 158, 159
the Imaginary 114, 115, 116–117
injury 40, 177–178, 180, 181, 183–184
irregularity 65
Iverson, Allen 44

Jackson, Michael 121
Jacobs, Ted 130
James, C. L. R. 16
James, LeBron 115, 135–137, 142
James, William 100
Jeter, Derek 31, 115
John, Tommy 31, 122n1
Jones, E. 63
Joyce, Joan 28

Kansas City Cowboys 95
Katz, Howard M. 144–160
Keeley, S. 170–171
Kennedy, Teddy Jr. 53
Kimmelman, Michael 31
King, Billie Jean 82
Kinsella, W. P. 21–22
Klein, Melanie 120
Kohut, H. 114, 119–120, 128–129, 137
Kosslyn, Stephen M. 88
Koufax, Sandy 42, 97
Kristeva, J. 12, 15, 27

L. A. Galaxy 120
labor 17, 20
Lacan, J. 114, 116–117
Lacanian theory 12, 15
lacrosse 56
Lambert, Elizabeth 112
language 12, 22–26, 32
Laplanche, J. 114, 117, 118
Latin Americans 26
law 41
A League of Their Own (1992) 28
Lelyveld, Joe 99
Leonard, Kawhi 134, 141, 142
lesbians 28
liminality 66
Lincoln, Abraham 21
Lippmann, Paul 59
Littlefield, Bill 60n3
Lombardi, Vince 45, 115
losing: dejection 57; depression 63; emotions 53; impact on fans 2, 4–5, 6, 8n2; learning how to lose 55; therapy with adolescent 135–137
loss 129, 130, 147, 149, 158
loyalty 44, 45
lying 40

madness 95
Madonna 31
Malamud, Bernard 15
male gaze 15
Malinowski, Bronislaw 98
mania 2
Mantle, Mickey 47, 58–59
marathon running 176–186
Martin, G. L. 171
masculinity 16, 18, 19, 26, 28, 32, 57, 116
masochism 17, 18, 19
Mazilli, Lee 31
McCovey, William 77n7
McEnroe, John 80, 81, 86, 127–128
McLuhan, Marshall 37
media 45–46, 47
medication 166
Medwick, Ducky 13, 33n3
memory 72–74, 157, 163
mentation 157
mimetic rivalry 118–119
mindfulness 170
mirror neurons 73
mirror phase 115
Mitchell, Steve 89–91
Modell, A. 157

money 38, 45
mood 58, 151, 153; benefits of exercise 162, 164; impact of winning or losing on fans 2, 3–4, 5, 8n2; running 176
motor learning 144–145, 146, 155, 156–157
movement 88, 148, 149, 155, 158, 159
Munson, Thurman 30, 31
Musial, Stan 13, 32n2
music 60, 131, 158

Namath, Joe 59
narcissism 43, 118, 121; athletes' dreams 158–159; healthy 128; narcissistic gratification 56, 57; narcissistic identification 62; narcissistic injury 40, 149; narcissistic pathology 129; primary 137
narrative 70
Nastase, Ilie 80, 81
nationalism 6–7
neuroscience 73, 88
neutrality 165–166, 173
New England Patriots 45
New York Giants 2, 68, 72, 77n7
New York Jets 59
New York Mets 8n3, 29
New York Yankees 15, 25, 30, 58–59, 61n4, 77n7, 99
Newfield, Jack 96
newspapers 46
non-directivity 165–167
nostalgia 30, 48, 73, 76
NY Rangers 103, 104

ocnophils 11, 32
Oedipus Complex 70
older adults 164–165
O'Leary, John V. 161–175
Olympics 16, 17, 51
O'Malley, Walter 96
omnipotence 41, 62, 129, 131, 141
Oudin, Melanie 83
owners 45

pain 4, 177–178, 183–184, 185
Palmer, Jim 31
Panksepp, Jaak 156–157
parents 55, 112, 113, 115, 117–118, 121; athletes' dreams 146–147, 150–151, 159; idealization of parental self-object 128–130, 142; lack of maternal care 179, 184–185; paternal object 138–139, 141
passion 44, 52, 54, 62, 102–111, 113; baseball 73; Freud 60; identification 5, 103, 104–105, 106–107, 110
patriarchy 12, 15
Payson, Joan 29
peak performance 84–85, 87
perception 86–87
perfection 131, 141
performativity 116
Petrova, Nadia 83
Petrucelli, Jean 80–91
phallicism 39, 40
Phallus 115
phantasy 65
Philadelphia Eagles 2
philobats 11, 32
physical development 155–156
Pinsky, Robert 42
pitchers 68, 69, 71, 98
play 52–53, 58, 105, 108–109, 115, 119, 156–157
playfulness 47–48, 52
pleasure 12, 54
poker 40
Pollack, K. 170
postmodern feminism 15, 29
power 16
Pride of the Yankees (1942) 27
projective identification 106
psychoanalysis: aerobic exercise 162–163, 167–169, 170–171, 173; baseball comparison 65–66, 75–76, 77n4; dynamic shifts 70; engagement with culture 61n6; gender 29, 31–32; non-directivity 165–167; play 54; resistance 169–171; sports and 16, 19, 50, 51–52, 114–122; tennis 82; time 78n10
psychopharmacology 77n4, 166
puberty 130
punctuated equilibrium 77n6

race 6, 18, 26
radio 25–26, 45–46
Ramirez, Manny 33n9
rape survivors 168–169
regression 11–12, 30, 62
regularity 65–67, 72
Reifsteck, E. 172
relatedness 86
relaxation techniques 170

REM sleep 144, 146, 155, 156, 157
resistance 19, 168, 169–171, 173
reverie 76
Reynolds, Allie 98
Rice, Jim 74
Richardson, Bobby 77n7
risk taking 82, 84
rituals 98
rivalry 118–119, 136
Rizzutto, Phil 25, 26, 98
Robinson, Jackie 26, 30
Rodriguez, Alex 31
role models 127, 142
Roosevelt, Franklin 47
Rosenblatt, A. 165, 168
Rosenheck, Dan 26
Roth-Goldberg, Stephanie 176–186
Rowe, Dave 95
rules 60, 66, 67, 69, 75–76, 88
rumination 2, 4, 164
running 161–162, 171, 176–186
Rushdie, Salman 102
Ruth, Babe 21, 30

safety 66
Safina, Dinara 82
Sampras, Pete 80
Scalia, Antonin 51
scapegoating 118–119, 121–122
schemas 155, 157
schizophrenia 166
Schott, Marge 29
seduction 114, 117, 121
Seinfeld, Jerry 5
self-care 170, 177
self-concept 144
self, construction of 16
self-control 172
self-criticism 38–39, 81, 90, 180
self-efficacy 164, 172–173
self-esteem 57, 58, 119–120, 127; benefits of exercise 163, 164; identity 144; Kohut 128
self-harm 176–177, 178, 179, 180, 181
self-loathing 39
self-object relationships 119–120, 128–129, 137, 142
self-reflection 41
self-regulation 133, 176–177
self-states: group psychotherapy 104, 107, 109; running 177, 183; tennis 82, 83, 86, 87, 88
Seligman, Stephen 62–79, 103

sexual abuse 182
shame 39, 163, 180
Sharapova, Maria 83
Sheed, Wilfred 24
shirts, rooting for 5–6
Simmons, Ben 140, 141
situations 66–70
skiing 60
Slavin, Malcolm 59–60
Smiley, Jane 118
Smith-Marek, E. 168–169
Smith, Red 24
Snow, J. T. 68
soccer 17, 41; aerobic exercise 162; danger 60; fans 99–100, 102, 103; time 70
social constructivism 22–23
social media 142
Sorrentino, Gilbert 25
South Park 39–40
space 64–65, 86
"spechating" 37, 45–48
spectacle 18, 20, 41, 46, 47–48, 72
splitting 47
sportsmanship 53, 80, 119
St. Louis, Martin 104
statistics 71–72
Staub, Rusty 30–31
Stengel, Casey 29, 34n10
Stephens-Davidowitz, S. 105–106
steroids 31, 43–44
street games 18
stress 164–165
strikes 22
structure 65–66, 76, 88
style 67
subjectivity 19, 115
suicidal ideation 108
Sullivan, Harry Stack 106
Super Bowl 2, 59
supervision 89–91
suspension of disbelief 40, 41
swimming 70, 162, 180
Switzer, Katherine 176
Szymanski, Stefan 113

talk shows 45–46
tennis 32, 80–91, 97–98, 127–128
Thomson, Bobby 77n3
time 17–18; baseball 20–22, 70–71, 74, 75; psychoanalysis 78n10; tennis 84–85, 86
Tkachuk, G. A. 171

tomboys 28, 29
track sports 17, 70, 161–162
transference 129, 165, 173; athletes' dreams 154, 159; fans 3; group psychotherapy 109; running 177
transitional space 37, 40, 47, 54, 58
trauma 168, 169, 176–177
treadmills 179–180
tribalism 6–7, 118

uncertainty 66–67, 69, 76, 98
unpredictability 72, 75

Vick, Michael 17, 33n6
Vilas, Guillermo 89
violence 7, 12, 62, 118–119
visual processing 86–87
visualization 87–88

Wade, Virginia 82
Wainwright, Loudon 39
walking 162, 171
Wallace, David Foster 37, 97–98

Walsh, R. 164, 165
watching 37
Watson, Robert 1, 102–111
weather conditions 69
Wellesley, Arthur 113–114
Whitman, 64
Williams, Serena 80, 81, 115
Williams, Ted 28, 34n12
Winnicott, D. W. 54, 90, 105, 108
winning 45, 57–58, 115; emotions 53; gracious 55; impact on fans 2, 4–5, 6, 8n2; therapy with adolescent 135–137
wish-fulfillment 159n1
women: athletic opportunities for 113; baseball 12–13, 14–15, 20, 21, 23, 27–29; fans 32; Olympics 17; running 176–186
words 22–26
worthlessness 178–179
Wrigley, Charles 28

Yalom, I. D. 106
youth sports 21, 113